CW00556478

# WHITEWAY COLONY

## The Social History of a Tolstoyan Community

# WHITEWAY COLONY

## The Social History of a Tolstoyan Community

JOY THACKER

Joy Thacker

First published in the United Kingdom 1993
by Joy Thacker, Fairhaven, Whiteway, Nr Miserden, Stroud, Glos.



ISBN 0 9521760 0 9

Produced by Alan Sutton Publishing Ltd, Stroud, Glos.
Printed in Great Britain

# CONTENTS

For Leonie
and all Whiteway people past and present.

# ACKNOWLEDGEMENTS

During your reading, you will find the name Gassy mentioned, and to this unique person, whom I saw but never met, as he died a year after our arrival at Whiteway, I cannot convey enough thanks. Oh that he were here now for me to talk with, what a wonderful thing that would be! Instead he has left his mark, conveyed through his small spidery writing, providing a wealth of interest, which has spurred me into greater exploration, compelling me to write.

Thank you to my daughter Vicky, who has contributed a chapter on her childhood experiences here in the 1970's and guided me with her knowledge of publishing.

Dear Leonie, sadly now no longer with us, thank you for answering all my questions with such honesty and wit, to see you was always a treat and a tonic, without your marvellous memory and patience this book would not be what it is. Also to Hilda, for her continued enthusiasm and interest, Joy and Peter, and Elsie Johnson who always made time to listen, and to Sue Everson from Alan Sutton Publishing who sorted me out.

I am also grateful to Elizabeth Skinner and Sheepscombe History Group, for allowing the use of the Carmen Maurice diary, an added extra which makes such thrilling reading.

Three more important people in my life deserve special mention. My son, for rushing to my aid when the computer took on its own mind, my daughter Katrina for producing several photographs and designing the jacket, my husband Keith, who copied and re-copied endless photographs, a tedious task not always welcomed just because the light was right and the photos were available.

Finally, grateful thanks are offered to all those who have contributed photographs, information, or simply just encouragement. I did begin to make a list but there were so many names that the risk of missing someone out was too great, but you will all know who you are and most of you are mentioned throughout the chapters of this book on our community, Whiteway Colony, which I hope you will all enjoy.

The sources referred to during the compilation of this book are the Whiteway Archives, Gassy's writings, Freedom Centenary magazine, the Carmen Maurice diary, photographs from colonists, and information gathered from many many conversations.

# Introduction

Although this book has been written by me, it is not really mine but Whiteway Colony's. I am but a conveyor of its events, recorded through letters, meetings and memories of many who have racked their brains in order to compile it.

Stories retold throughout the years often times have blurred, or been misinterpreted, and my task here is to represent them clearly and truthfully, in order that misunderstandings may be rectified and other facts understood.

This book is a glimpse into the Community's social and historical life as seen through those principally involved with it in that particular age.

Whiteway is not only unique in that it was a Colony with Tolstoyan origins or indeed of any other denomination, be it anarchist or religious, but in its very survival. The basis on which it evolved has changed little, the acreage of land remains the same, as does its land holding and administration system. It has escaped the fate of other villages, consumed into the sprawl of suburbia, and remains amid farmland as it did practically a hundred years ago.

The land scheme introduced here was the result of the strong Tolstoyan influence which had become increasingly popular in England towards the end of the nineteenth century. The strong feelings which Tolstoy aroused in those who were already unhappy about the conditions in this country during that time, resulted in the formation of The Brotherhood Trust, which was designed to encourage the growth of societies endeavouring to promote, as far as they were able, those lessons he set forth.

It was envisaged that each society would ultimately purchase land where cultivation and voluntary co-operation would be its practice, together with caring towards one another, as seen in Bible teachings though not necessarily religious, being of a more practical nature.

Other people through contact with them would, it was hoped, set up similar organisations and live likewise, so causing a network to be formed, which as it multiplied would influence the entire country, delivering it from those capitalists which they all detested.

The innovator behind the Brotherhood Trust scheme was Bruce Wallace, who began one at Southgate Road in London in 1891. Some of the changes he envisaged were fair wages, trade unions, and sickness and old-age benefits.

John Colman Kenworthy also felt similarly after reading Tolstoy's articles while on his way to America in 1890. In fact it completely enveloped his life causing him to throw himself wholeheartedly into all things concerning it.

This led him to combine with Wallace in his Brotherhood Trust Scheme. He involved himself with writing articles and lecturing and visits to those Brotherhood Churches which had sprung up near and far.

The purchase of land was of great importance according to Tolstoy. In his article entitled 'How Shall We Escape', published in 1901, he writes of the unfairness of the rich owning land on which crops are produced for them by overworked labourers who do all the work for a pittance, while the landlords rake in the profits, with never a finger dirtied in the soil which they own. I quote,

> Everywhere labourers overwork themselves for idle rich landlords. They suffer from rupture, asthma, consumption, drink in despair and die before their time . . .
>
> And everywhere those for whom they work indulge in horses and carriages and pet dogs, conservatoires and games, from one year to another; each day from morning till evening, dressing as if for a holiday, playing eating and drinking, as not one of those who work for them could do, even on holiday.
>
> Why is this?
>
> The first answer that presents itself to the rural labourer is that it is owing to the land having been taken from him, and given to those who do not work it. So that the working either has no land, or so little that he cannot support himself or his family on it, and that he must either starve, or rent the land adjoining his own but possessed by those who do not work it; to rent it consenting of necessity to whatever terms are demanded. . . .

He continues,

> It is not merely want of land which causes the labourer to become enslaved to the rich; the causes are to be found also in the taxes and the high prices charged for the necessaries of life.
>
> . . . every man that is born has the same right to support himself from the land as he has the right to air or the sunlight; and that therefore no man has the right to regard any land he does not cultivate as his own, or to prevent others from cultivating it.
>
> But no Government will sanction this freedom, for most of the individuals who form the Government are land-owners; and on the possession of this property is based their existence. They know this, and hold tight to their privilege, and defend it.
>
> So it is evident that the slavery of the working classes will never be abolished while Governments continue.

Later he states,

> Every attempt of the working men to take possession of the land belonging to private owners will certainly end as it always ended, by soldiers coming and punishing and dispersing those who are endeavouring to get the land. Every attempt to avoid paying taxes will also end in the same way.

He concludes,

> If only men would apply their energies, not to external results but to that which causes these results – to their own life – then the power of violence and evil which at present holds and afflicts humanity would melt like wax before the fire.

Some of the Brotherhood Churches managed to buy land, others didn't. Whiteway was the second attempt by those connected with the Brotherhood Church at Croydon, and when the first one at Purleigh perished, those interested in its principles went to Whiteway instead.

Strangely, for all of its set-backs and hardships this community remains very much in existence, as the rest of the book will prove.

Whiteway has been the target of numerous stories throughout its life, many springing from hardly anything at all, and the people here have become used to them. Most myths have an element of truth in them but sadly they can overshadow other, more interesting and worthwhile aspects of the colony.

The only other book about Whiteway Colony was written by Nellie Shaw in 1935. It describes the strong feelings that accumulated over the four years preceding its formation, which eventually culminated in its birth.

As Nellie's book is the only record so far, and covers only thirty years, then it is time that another one should be available to include more recent events. I am sure that Nellie would not object to the early years being related once more, albeit from a different viewpoint which has been gained from the passing of years and Whiteway archive material, which I am grateful to have at my disposal.

I will stress that while the book is completely accurate concerning its dates and content, if by some chance a minor incident concerning any individual is slightly awry, then I can be forgiven.

Joy Thacker,<br>
Whiteway Colony, England.<br>
February 1993.

# *Chapter 1*

# PURLEIGH COLONY – THE ORIGINS OF WHITEWAY

Whiteway Colony was intended, at its formation, to be revolutionary and to some degree has remained so up to the present day.

Based partly on Tolstoyan views, with their teachings of freedom, equality, self government and brotherhood, and a strong anti-government inclination with its enforced rules and the domination and fear which it invariably carries with it, then the combined result proved from its very conception that it would be watched and criticised by those with more conventional inclinations.

Still in Queen Victoria's reign, with restrictions and rigidity, it could be said that the Whiteway pioneers were foolish to attempt such a wild experiment. It was a time when the woman's place was definitely within the home, governed by a set of etiquettes no-one of any standing should dare to venture from. To do so affected the whole family, bringing disrepute on all. The male of those times was allowed a stretching of wings, acceptable to society as part of their developement, but basically it was essential to maintain that respectable front. Those who refuted this knew undeniably that they risked their credibility regarding their future prospects.

So what ever were these intelligent young men and women doing by behaving in such an outrageous manner, forsaking their inborn principles and upbringing, to live in hardship high upon these Cotswold Hills? Their decision to adopt this unconventional life was not by any means arrived at overnight. Four years had elapsed since The Croydon Brotherhood Church's formation, the society from which their land scheme evolved. During that time many lessons had been learned and in this new attempt it was hoped to benefit from those lessons.

From the early Brotherhood gatherings where those disheartened with the social climate in the world could meet amid the company of others similarly minded grew a strong commitment. There was this longing to branch out and to physically do something themselves about it, to prove what they preached.

The capitalism which they were convinced was a crippling disease upon the country, with its class structure, and resulting fetters on life would have to change, for surely all humanity should be able to avail themselves freely of all things, without restraint or restriction whatever their circumstances? It

*Count Leo Nikolayevich Tolstoy. Born in Yasnaya Polyana, in the province of Tula in 1828. He resented all efforts to organise the external conditions of mens' lives, which he was certain ultimately affected their inner self. Therefore, small communities consisting of free men, close to nature was his vision.*

was possible they were convinced, of their ability to obtain happiness now on earth not in some far distant future, if they all worked together freely and honestly, respecting each others views in mutual co-operation. They felt sure that their example would cause others to adopt similar communities, which would ultimately change society for the better.

So this was the framework of Whiteway. As you read this book about the activities of its first century and bear in mind that government by law, country or church were to them all constrictive organisations, then you will see why deeds, coinage, voting, tithe and marriage, were sometimes opposed, and not made an issue of just to shock the watchers. It must also be remembered that as the policy was for each individual to act freely according to his inclinations, then not all were expected to be united in their views. One might be inclined to his religion, then properly he should visit his church. Another might feel that he must support his country in its efforts during wartime. Then he should feel able to sign up. This decision would be an alternative one to that felt passionately by his neighbour, when to take a life was a totally alien and unthinkable thing, and even imprisonment was preferable to its enforcement. All these were equally acceptable. Everyone could, if committed to the welfare of his fellow man, live side by side peaceably and happily.

This new land settlement was put here to prove it to all, and hopefully encourage others to do the similar thing. Misunderstandings were expected, and those early settlers from previous experience were accustomed to them, for the few who set up this colony had not come to this as novices. Most had served in varying degrees in similar projects in other parts of the country.

The Croydon Brotherhood Church was formed by six young Socialists at 46 Tamworth Road in 1894. They were Mary Grover, Nellie Shaw, Fred Muggeridge, William Gilruth, and James and Frank Henderson. It was from there that the seed grew for Purleigh Colony, the society's first land experiment, based on lines very similar to that of its offshoot community, Whiteway, People were drawn to the Croydon Brotherhood because anyone, whoever they were, could speak on any subject they felt was of importance, and whatever its content, they would be given a hearing. At the Sunday afternoon and evening meetings, an inspired lecture on controversial social matters would be given by John Colman Kenworthy, a former member of the Ruskin Society in Liverpool, and author of *The Anatomy of*

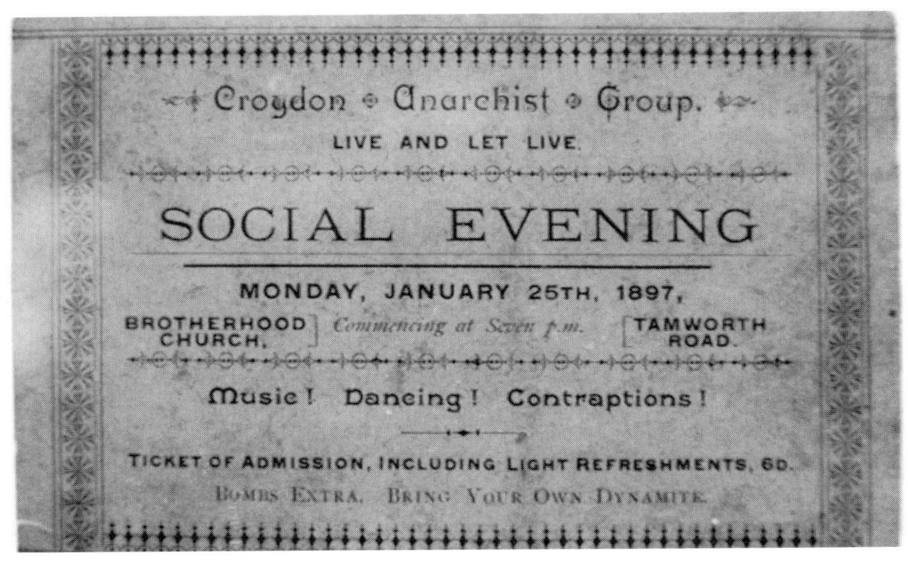


*Jeannie Straughan's unused admission card. A rare piece of Whiteway's history.*

*Misery*, which was prompted after living amongst the poor and wanting to do something about it.

He was the main instigator of the Brotherhood who, with his powerful oratory and eventual meeting with the great Tolstoy, was able to draw in those of similar mind. This, combined with relevant literature on sale to back it up, and Labour songs from the Labour Church Hymn Book resulted in the Croydon Brotherhood Church becoming very popular.

As the membership increased, then plenty of people were available to voluntarily run a vegetarian store, called The Brotherhood Trust which opened on November 10th 1894. This was situated at 2 Hollycombe, Pitlake, West Croydon, being only a few minutes walk away from their premises at Tamworth Road. Its opening hours were from 7–10 pm. There was a basement room beneath the shop which stocked Labour and Tolstoyan papers and writings, and this became a reading room for those wishing to study their message. This literature could similarly be purchased by the public in the shop above. In January 1895, *The Brotherhood Intelligence*, a monthly paper, was begun by Kenworthy who had recieved personal permission from Tolstoy himself to translate his works. Among other items of relevent interest *The Intelligence* issued regular reports on the progress of many other similar groups which had begun to spring up both at home and abroad, all of whom had views and aims akin to those at Croydon. In fact it proved so popular that by the following September a printing press was bought, on which some members who were printers by trade voluntarily produced the ever expanding copies. The paper changed it's name as it doubled in size, to become *The New Order*.

In addition, a large house at Waddon built originally as a hotel was acquired by the Brotherhood and run as a hostel by Frank Henderson and his wife. This became known as Brotherhood House, opening its doors on 5 November. By the following March, the store had been transferred there, much enlarged, and managed by an ex-army captain. Two businesses were also begun. One of these was a tailoring enterprise with Drover and McDonald, which lasted until 1896 when Drover joined the Purleigh Colony, and McDonald formed a free-union, the other was Nellie Shaw's Reform Dressmaking project, both run on non-capitalist lines.

Aymler Maude with Vladimir Tchertkof, both Russian exiles and friends of Tolstoy, and their families joined the Brotherhood group at this time, and many stimulating discussions were held between them regarding the actual difficulties of living the type of life that Tolstoy envisaged. Regardless of this, the next step, the purchase of land and the formation of a farm colony, was taken. Readers of the September issue of *The New Order* were invited to join in this scheme by writing to the secretary of the group, S. Hopwood.

Suitable land was found just a few weeks later in Essex about a mile from the village of Purleigh, and five minutes walk from the nearby hamlet of Cocklarks. There were ten acres. William Sinclair, William Sudbury Protheroe and Hubert Hammond, three men wanting to be involved in the new scheme, volunteered to go there ahead of the others to get it ready for when they followed along a few months later. They lived frugally on about 5s a week, in a cottage at Cocklarks rented for £8 a year, and worked hard.

By the following Spring when they were joined by the others, they had achieved an amazing amount with at least three acres of land having been dug, half an acre to a depth of three feet, in readiness for the planting of an orchard the following autumn. The constitution which had been drawn up twice by a young lawyer, the first being rejected because it seemed too socialistic, never needed to be adhered to, so proving that its important point of co-operative labour must have been carried out to the satisfaction of everyone there.

That April William Hone, the colonists' gardening friend moved with his wife, daughter Maude and three sons, into one of the colony's rented houses, half an hour's walk away from the Colony. With them came two goats and six fowl. His advice had been invaluable during those early months, and the intention was for him and his family to occupy a house which was being built communally on the Colony land, constructed out of bricks made on site, involving a lot of hard work and requiring many helpers. The Hones were eventually able to move into their new home the Wednesday before Christmas 1897. The debris surrounding it was cleared during the holidays, allowing flower beds to be planted in its place.

The following February a house-warming was held in this completed house, with music, dancing and poetry readings. Also around this time a

*Cultivating land on either Purleigh or Whiteway in the late 1890's. The treeless landscape makes Whiteway the probable location. During December of Whiteway's first year apple, plum and pear trees were planted in trenches in the clay soil on the sloping land near the sheep dip. Also strawberries, with those involved having visions of a bumper harvest the following June.*

cow shed was completed ready to house the two cows that were due a few days later. This added to the already completed stable, since occupied with a pony, the coal sheds, a one-hundred-foot partly-heated greenhouse planted with grape vines and tomato plants and a workshop 20ft by 10ft long. There were also fowl houses, accommodating over forty hens, successfully hatched in an incubator made by Sinclair, two goats and a swarm of bees. This and much more had been achieved and very impressive it all sounds.

*The New Order* meanwhile continued to carry regular reports on the progress of this farm experiment. Hubert Hammond on the 14 March 1898 wrote,

> We have no rules, each one is left to do as he or she likes, held in check only by their own good sense, and the general opinion of his comrades. Neither have we any fixed rules about the admission of new members. Some have brought money with them, others have not. Usually we try to give people wishing to join a clear statement of our position, and leave it to them to decide whether they will cast in their lot with us to work towards the ideal or not. That ideal is to live lives worthy of men; to endeavour more and more to develop tolerance and unselfishness, and to work earnestly for a time when we can welcome all who care to come. At present that time seems a long time off.

After eighteen months Purleigh had fourteen colonists and many regular visitors and helpers. A visitor writes,

> There is no reason for keeping up appearances, they do not count. So people here dress as they please, and behave as they please, and nobody objects. It might be feared that on the removal of restraints all sorts of extravagances would break out, but so far I have seen nothing very alarming, while social intercourse gains greatly by being enabled to rise above the trivial things that so often drag it down to boredom.

Many came to stay with ideas of joining. One of these was Arnold Eiloart, a conscientious objector from Denmark. He generously contributed all his recently inherited money to Purleigh, so enabling the land to be extended by a further thirteen acres. John Kenworthy came also, building himself a house with assistance from some friends from Yorkshire, who had formed themselves into a building co-operative. Aymler Maude and his family arrived soon after, renting a house nearby in which he made numerous colonists welcome.

Then during Easter 1898, a newcomer arrived at Purleigh. He was

Samuel Bracher, a member of the Society of Friends and a journalist from Gloucester. His pockets and conscience were weighted down with £1,000 of inherited money which he had not earned, so felt he should not have. He spent several months at Purleigh trying to decide if he would join them and give his money to the furtherance of their venture. His mind was eventually made up for him in July, when the colony refused to allow two young men to join them. They were Jack Bent and Owen Trafford, both tradesmen from the Midlands. This caused Samuel and some of the others to rethink their future regarding the Purleigh Colony. Was not the purpose of this Colony to provide for anyone, regardless of what or whom they were? Samuel's views on such matters were so important to him that he abandoned all plans concerning Purleigh. With the support of the others, he decided to look for some other land on which to spend his money where a new, freer community could be set up by them and run in their own way.

The West of England Land Society at Gloucester was consulted over available land for this new scheme through Samuel's friend, Joseph Burtt, and soon a letter was received from Charlie Fox, one of its members, telling of land for sale in Herefordshire. All those interested in joining Samuel's new group assembled at Charlie Fox's house in Clarence Street, ready to ride on bicycles the following day to Herefordshire to see this land for themselves. Those involved in the search were Joe Burtt, William Sinclair, Nellie Shaw, Arnold Eiloart, Jack Bent, Samuel Bracher and Lottie Dunn.

Disappointingly the Herefordshire land was unsuitable, and so after deciding to make the best of a bad situation, they rode the longer way back via Painswick, Sheepscombe, Bisley and Minchinhampton where those who were able to spare the time stayed for the remainder of the weekend.

It took two months for land suited to their requirements to be found, but during that time Samuel had fallen in love with Lottie Dunn, a former governess to Aymler Maude's children. In fact it was not only Lottie that had won his love, but also the pretty, nearby village of Sheepscombe, which caused his initial enthusiasm concerning the farm land experiment to dwindle. He really now wanted to settle down in that nearby village with Lottie.

This turn of events worried the other members of the new group, causing them to think that if they did not find land soon then Samuel's interest in the Farm Scheme would disappear entirely, and their dreams of a new community would come to nothing.

So it was to their great relief that on 13 September 1898, Joe Burtt wrote to them from Gloucester to report that part of a nearby estate was up for sale and he thought would suit them very well.

He writes,

Dear Nellie, 41 acres of land at £7 an acre, fairly good and very suitable in most ways, one and a half miles from here and with road frontage, plenty of water, cottage £150. The owner has given us the refusal for a week and we hope Hone will come down to see it. I do feel very pleased and thankful that it has all gone so well.

This land was to become Whiteway Colony!

# Chapter 2
# THE PIONEERS

All the pioneers were educated people, many with a profession and a fine future ahead, which they were prepared to abandon in order to fulfil an inner need of reformation.

Sudbury Protheroe, at the age of twenty-four would, without doubt, have had a promising future in his family auctioning business at Leytonstone in Essex, had he remained there as a junior partner, gaining experience steadily and working his way up eventually to the dizzy heights of success, with all the benefits that would inevitably bring. Yet he threw it all in to join two land schemes of uncertain stability.

It is supposed that his family considered this episode in his life as a temporary fling, a time of rebellion against conventionality, with normality

*Sudbury Protheroe. The traditional clothes, as worn in this photograph were replaced by shorts, sandals and shirts (bare chests if the weather was hot). On Friday 16 July 1901, Sud was summoned to Stroud Court and charged with indecency, following a meeting on the public road at Whiteway with the Rev Herbert Edgecumbe Hadow, curate of Bisley, while on his way to the spring, clad only in shorts. He was fined 10s, which was going to be paid by friends as it was during the no-money period, however, it was actually paid by the vicar himself who was doubtless feeling guilty after thinking the matter over.*

*Jeannie Straughan. The long skirts and stays, common at the start of this century were replaced by loose, short frocks, without sleeves or belts. Hair was worn loose and the only hats were sun-bonnets.*

being resumed as age and sense took over. They were to be proved wrong for he remained firmly at Whiteway until, on reaching the age of sixty, the urge to try something different overcame him once again, and he moved to Salisbury to begin another phase in his life, as the owner of a shop, where he sold his wonderful home-made fudges and vegetarian foods. He was to prove that although a bad manager regarding his financial affairs, with money holding little interest for him, when it came to creating a product, as with his breads and confectionary, he was indeed a perfectionist.

Jeannie Straughan lived at Whiteway until she died in May 1950 at the age of eighty-one. She and Sudbury, or Sud, had met at Purleigh, and on settling at Whiteway had united together in a free union relationship, living for a while in Whiteway House. She had formerly been a member of the Croydon Brotherhood Church and a member of the Purleigh Colony. In her occupation as governess, she had taught the children of Aymler Maude, a translator and Russian exile from Moscow who, after staying for a short while at Brotherhood House, soon came to live near the Purleigh settlement. As their views on most issues were similar, they all became close friends and invitations for meals and social discussions became a common occurrence from then on. Jeannie was a kind person and an accomplished pianist, entertaining the Colonists for many years with concerts at her home.

William Sinclair, a Scotsman from Wick in Caithness, was of a completely

*William Sinclair with Rachelle, taken around 1907.*

opposite disposition from Sud. He was older, being thirty-five on coming to Whiteway, still single, and as experienced as anyone could be on land settlements, with two others already tucked safely under his belt.

A few years previously William had abandoned the security of his job as a bank clerk, and with a partner who soon left him, had tried to live an alternative type of existence on a piece of land in Suffolk. Purleigh tempted him to try again, and there he was once more in at the start.

Similarly, Whiteway came along two years later, and here he was again, working from dawn to dusk, always around to offer sound advice, a pillar of strength, and a rock amid the turmoil. He died at Whiteway, not as a grand old man, tired of life and needing a well earned rest, but at the mere age of sixty-five, in a fall at his home from which he never recovered.

Another pioneer who played a major role during Whiteway's first year but had to leave when his father became ill, and so only visited from then on, was Joseph Burtt. It must have taken some courage for him to embark on such a controversial experiment, for his very roots were steeped in respectability, his grandfather being the founder of the Gloucester Chamber of Commerce.

Joe himself had been a Bank Manager at Cheltenham, and for one who had held such a position of authority to be seen by former clients, wearing rolled up trousers and heavy boots, digging land just a few miles from home, must have cast doubts as to his sanity.

*Arnold Eiloart.*

His views on capitalism had changed dramatically a little while earlier when he became involved with Charles Fox, a prominent socialist and Sam Bracher, both of whom were members of an organisation called The West of England Land Society and The Gloucester Society of Friends.

After a brief stay at Purleigh, he took part in the finding and procuring of the ground for the new Whiteway scheme. So accordingly with his considerable financial knowledge, he undertook any transactions and money matters, becoming Whiteway's unofficial first treasurer.

Arnold Eiloart was involved with Whiteway Colony for seven years, yet he only lived on its land for the first nine months, and within this time he unwittingly caused a trauma that influenced its entire future. He had been a Purleigh member, joining their group after leaving Denmark as a conscientious objector. While there he had bought them thirteen acres of land adjoining the ten they already owned, animals and equipment. Even then he still managed to contribute to a fund set up to help in the removal of the Doukhobors from Caucasia, near the Russia–Turkey border, to begin a new life in Cyprus and Canada.

Their opposition to some of the laws and regulations of the Russian administration and disapproval of the orthodox church, together with their refusal to comply with the newly introduced military service, caused imprisonment, torture and exiling. Tolstoy, after learning of their plight, sent the following proposal to those at Caucasia,

> Never serve any military service, because war is sacrilegious to the divine man; divide your possessions equally among you; never eat meat; collect all the firearms which they possess and openly burn them. The burning of the guns would be the symbol of the break by the Doukhobors from the old world.

This very philosophy has permeated throughout Whiteway's history, from the burning of their deeds to the objection to war. Arnold Eiloart, as a Doctor of Philosophy intellectually and in practice was one of the strongest upholders of Tolstoy's principles, living for many years without the use of money, even though through his past involvement with it, he had proof of its power and what it could achieve. He struggled on for several years in this manner avoiding its use in a variety of inventive ways. However finally, after leaving the atmosphere of the Colony, and married with a growing family to support, he once more succumbed to its use, and began to earn his living again in the more conventional ways of teaching and writing.

One wonders if his sense of dress changed also, for he had been accustomed to wearing his trousers up to his knees and sandals on his feet which, combined with his mane of hair and matching moustache, made him a figure not easily forgotten to those unused to such attire.

The only 'couple' among those early settlers was May and Mac. They had been associated with the Croydon Brotherhood Church, and already had a

*Nellie Shaw taken in 1938. Nellie's book on Whiteway's early days was available in twelve countries. Its effect was twofold, with those in the surrounding district of Whiteway gaining more understanding of the colonists and their ways, while those actually living there had mixed feelings with some critisizing her for not mentioning people she disliked, and leaving out completely events with which she disagreed. In a letter to Gassy in 1936 she writes 'it's certain I could have filled another volume with such stories (those about colonists) and perhaps been a best seller' . . . 'By Jove, though, I could tell some funny ones'.*

small daughter Katherine, with a son Keith, being born almost immediately after they arrived. Their happiness seemed complete but was sometimes marred by moodiness on Mac's part, and then it did not take much to arouse his temper. May shouldered all the responsibility for food and womanly tasks during those early months, although ably assisted by everyone there as the occasion arose.

As all were vegetarians, meals consisted of porridge, nuts, rice, wheat, pulses and home-grown vegetables. No one drank alcohol, but some did smoke occasionally.

Nellie Shaw was one of the four early settlers who remained on Whiteway all her life. She was a member of The Croydon Brotherhood, but never actually progressed on to become a Purleigh Colonist. This was not because she was not interested in it and its progress, for she spent as much time there as she could, but her involvement with her revolutionary dress making concern at the Brotherhood House, run on a fair pay, non-profit-making, eight-hour day, took up her time. On her realisation that even this improved situation was far from the ideal, with only those with money able to afford the finished result, and those with a real need doing without as before, she decided to abandon the entire idea and join the others in their new land venture.

She eventually arrived at Whiteway fully six months after its formation, and even then she was unable to sleep on the Colony, but rented instead a cottage two miles away at Climperwell, where she remained for two years, settling at last on Whiteway ground in 1901.

So here they are, with the common aim to share, work, love and build a united community, free from restraint and injustice. We will now look into its progression.

## *Chapter 3*

# The Bracher Breakup

Although everyone was united and of one mind in the aims of their future venture, when Sam changed his mind and decided to stay in Sheepscombe with Lottie, leaving the others to embark on the farm scheme in their own way, problems began to arise immediately. Doubtless he felt he had let them down, and an element of guilt may have crept in, for the large capital which he had promised and which their future plans had revolved around, had now to be reduced by half, for he needed the rest for his own affairs.

He was basically an unselfish man and generous to a fault given his choice to sacrifice an enormous fortune, that many in a similar position, would have used to better their own ends. But the situation from his viewpoint had now changed, and he was in love and influenced by that love and the woman to whom it was extended. This had caused him to deviate from the initial urgency and excitement of his original enterprise, and to choose another course, which not only affected him, but was bound to rebound on the others also. As he did not wish to let his fellow men down completely, then he had no other alternative but to allow them to continue on without him in the manner they thought fit.

His respectable background, without doubt made him a man of honour, for his family owned a successful draper's business in Wincanton, Somerset. Later, while in Gloucester serving his apprenticeship in journalism with John Bellows, he had joined the Society of Friends. He struck up a friendship there with Joe Burtt, himself a man of integrity, who remained his trusted friend throughout all the turmoil that unbeknown to them lay ahead.

In a letter to Nellie, Joe writes,

> Things had for a long time been in a very vague condition and one morning Sam and I went into accounts and he said he would like each group, Whiteway and Sheepscombe to have about half, so we worked that out roughly and found it would leave us with about £100 for keeping us till crops come in and for working the land. When the matter was laid before the meeting, of course it came as a shock when we had expected to build and do various other things. . . . The feeling left by the meeting resulted in a sort of cloud which hung over us separating particularly Sam and Lottie from us, but I think they made an effort to break through it and both came to a business meeting which I

*Whiteway House taken before the addition of a downstairs window overlooking the road. This was undertaken when the Portlocks were there. It seems incredible that such a modest cottage could house so many people.*

got together last Thursday. After I had read a list of our wants Sam said what he wished to do, that was, gave [*sic*] us the balance of money to make up our half of the original capital.

In addition, he wrote,

He spoke nicely and said how sorry he was that any vagueness on his part should have mislead [*sic*] us. He is a dear boy as you know well . . . Altogether it was a great relief to get the affair settled and now we have £125 on hand, and when we have paid our bills and bought the trees for the orchard we shall have about £65 to keep us till our crops come and generally run the show. What do you think of that, but it doesn't bother me now I know where we are.

Meanwhile the Whiteway group had managed to sort their sleeping arrangements out for, with the cottage being too small to house them all, other rented accommodation was acquired at Bidfield Cottages and Climperwell, near the farm.

Both groups were unanimous in their interpretations regarding the administration of the land at least. They did not want one owner, for this surely was the main objection to the life surrounding them, and from which they were rebelling. Their aim was for it to be available to those who felt as they did. No constitution was drawn up, as constrictive views were alien to these principles, for all felt that the rule of right and wrong would reign when nurtured in the atmosphere of trust. Unfortunately for them, one of the most constrictive and damaging forms of ruling bodies could not be avoided entirely. Almost at once they stumbled upon it and their consciences were tested.

By law, deeds have to be signed when exchange occurs between the seller and the buyer. It is an unavoidable hazard and refusal to acquiesce means no deal, and therefore in their case, no land. But no one wanted to be the one to sign.

Eventually they decided the only remedy was for several to sign together, so making it a joint affair. Joe, who was accustomed to such things because of his past occupation and Sinclair, together with Sud, all signed together. The legality was dispensed with, but for a scheme based on anarchistic lines, it seemed an inexpedient start. So to prove that deeds held no importance anyway, and that by destroying them they would rid themselves of past ties and influences, they spiked the papers on a pitchfork, smeared them with paraffin and burnt them. The proof of their purchase, with the begrudgingly inscribed signatures had disintegrated to a pile of ashes, and to them their land was released from conventionality, liberated, for them to use in the form that they felt was acceptable.

Sam and Lottie, although on holiday sent word of their approval of this flamboyant act and even suggested that they might join them when they returned. When they did visit Whiteway as promised, Sam offered Joe further financial assistance immediately, and for later if needed, a gesture which was taken up then and there, as their meagre funds were decreasing rapidly. All seemed harmonious at last, but this was to prove short lived.

May and Mac split up. Mac's quick temper had finally consumed him, and after a last outburst had stormed back to London, leaving May and their two babies. When he remained away, she rented a small cottage at Wishanger, a hamlet just a short distance away across the fields, where she settled with her children. She continued to contribute towards the practical side of the colony's needs, with repairing and making clothes, a task much more in her line than land work anyway.

A friendship which had developed with Arnold Eiloart, now deepened, and when it was obvious that Mac's departure was permanent, Arnold moved from Whiteway House to be with her at Wishanger. Trouble flared up when Sud and Eiloart saw Mac in London, while on a walking trip in July, which resulted typically, in Mac losing his head and storming back to Whiteway to confront May. This very act was to influence Whiteway's entire future, for it triggered off all the latent emotions which had lain dormant between the two groups.

On the Colonists' adamant refusal to turn Eiloart and May out, as Sam and his associates thought they should do, then John Kenworthy himself came down from Purleigh, in an effort to instil some sense into them. His condemning sermon made little difference, as all felt that what an individual chose to do was their affair, whether it was right or wrong. As journalists, and knowing the power of the written word, Sam and Kenworthy wrote letters to the local papers, relating to all in the district around the misdemeanours of those new settlers upon the hills, and of their immorality.

Sam had made many friends in Sheepscombe, all of whom knew that it was he who had been the benefactor of this new experiment, and his feelings of being let down. It was obvious that something constructive was needed, so Sam requested a meeting with the contentious settlers to try to resolve the situation. As Joe and Sinclair were both absent, the Colonists asked if the meeting might wait until they returned, but Sam was so distracted that he wanted to hold it right away.

It therefore took place on the evening of Friday, 25 August 1899 in the rick yard at Whiteway. The meeting should have been at seven, but it was nearer eight o'clock when Sam and Lottie eventually arrived, the transport for them and their many friends being supplied by J.G.K. Partridge of Sheepscombe. They were also accompanied by four policemen, co-opted from the surrounding villages of Bisley, Painswick and Birdlip, and two reporters, to ensure that no small detail would be missed.

Surprisingly, Whiteway was not short on back-up. A fair assortment of relatives, visitors, and even some neighbours, were there to see fair play, all sitting comfortably on the ground in the balm of the evening.

*The Stroud Journal* writes on 1 September 1899,

> Gathered in the rick yard were all sorts of conditions of men, from those holding university degrees to able bodied sea men. Women too, were also in evidence and the utter lack of conventionality in the attire of both sexes, gave a most picturesque effect to the whole scene. Bare legs and heads, and feet covered only with sandals of the ancients were prominent; while some of the women were very quaintly dressed.

While waiting for Sam, Jack Bent whose voice was a credit to him in both tone and volume, had led them in community singing, to while away the time, and the two colony cows in the field over the wall contentedly chewed on their cud. When Lottie was seated in her chair, Sam was ready to address the gathering.

He emphasised that he did not want to quarrel with anyone, for whether they had done right or wrong was not really his affair. He was really there to sort the business side of the situation out. He had observed their efforts since they had been in operation over the last year, and as far as could be seen, nothing of what they had set out to do had been achieved. He had thought that the aims of this new way of life here was to live in such a way that their neighbours near, and perhaps even further would benefit from their example, and hopefully wish to take that same road for themselves. This had not happened at all. Instead, they had done nothing, and indeed were viewed by some as immoralists. He felt they had done much damage.

This outcome had upset him, for he had trusted them, and they had let him down and wasted his money. Not only that, they had succeeded in making him and others who had assisted them look foolish. He felt it was now his responsibility to sort it out, not only for himself, but for those others also.

During the months they had lived there, he had paid for the land, given money for food, bought tools, and physically assisted when he was able. He knew that there was no chance of getting his money back, but he would like his land, and the things on it which he had paid for!

Sud said that the land was not theirs to give, so could not be returned. He thought that the best policy was to cultivate what they had, and endeavour to set a good example to the others who were to come. He had signed one document, and he certainly was not going to sign another!

As darkness fell, and many opinions by as many people had been extended, but a fit solution still note found, Tom Bell, a Whiteway supporter suggested an adjournment. Sam, seeing the cows nearby, declared that if he could not have his land back, then he would certainly take his cows, for he considered them his private property. Arthur Haliday and John Boulton led the cows away to Sheepscombe, where they were tied in Mr Partridge's stable, awaiting a purchaser. That night they were renamed, from Primrose and Leap Year to Liberty and Free Love.

The police remained in the Whiteway vicinity until one o'clock in the morning, but they need not have bothered, for no trouble ensued. The reporters did the job they came to do, with the whole confrontation faithfully recorded in the papers. Many people reading about it came up to Whiteway, to catch a glimpse of these strange new people for themselves.

In the 8 September issue of *The Weekly Press* Walter Woolham, a former colonist, spoke of his former comrades in a spirit of love and respect, and expressed the belief that the reports concerning the settlers at Whiteway had been somewhat exaggerated. He considered that Mr and Mrs Bracher and Mr Charles Fox had acted rather unwisely in publicly broadcasting the state of things at Whiteway, and thought it would have been better had the whole affair been settled quietly. If the latter course had been adopted the Colony would, in his opinion, have thrived although of course he could lose sight of the fact there were some people there from selfish motives, rather than for the noble and altruistic purposes they professed. He thought Mr Bracher was in the wrong in claiming the land after once giving it for the use of humanity. He added, 'It is probable that the Colony will go on for some time yet.'

Samuel during following years regained some of his money, but never retrieved the land, so leaving Whiteway to develop naturally into what it is today.

## *Chapter 4*

# WHITEWAY THROUGH THE EYES OF CARMEN MAURICE

Whiteway Colony was only one of several land experiments at this time in our history, but differed from some, being of socialist Tolstoyan origins. A depression in farming caused by a succession of bad harvests and the importation of cheap grain from abroad, had caused land owners, particularly those with large estates, to seek their livelihoods in the world of commerce and investment overseas, some even selling up completely to live abroad themselves. The tenant farmers, who had relied on their landlords to protect them from major catastrophe, now either abandoned farming to try another life in the world beyond or, with falling land and property prices, actually managed to buy their tenant farms from their landlord.

It is clear to see that land for sale was now widely available, and those who a few years before would never have contemplated owning even a small amount, were now able to purchase acres.

The land bought for the Whiteway scheme cost £7 an acre and was chosen mainly because of its existing cottage. This proved to be more important than first envisaged for, with only half the expected money available, none could be spared for building, as all income was needed just to live.

The crops did badly as the land was so exposed to the elements, with no trees to give the protection required especially for those leafy vegetables which grew above the soil. It is almost impossible to imagine how it was then compared with the Whiteway of today, for now the landscape is practically overrun with every conceivable type of tree and vegetation.

The shepherd's stone cottage, soon to become known as Whiteway House, belonged to the Hazel House, or Hasill House Estate, which was offered for sale in 1898. The land was divided into three portions of forty-one acres, eighty acres, and the balance which remained with the landowner's house.

The Whiteway farm group bought the forty-one acres; the adjoining eighty acres was sold to Farmer Causey ten months later.

After staying a month together at Sheepscombe while they renovated the cottage up to a habitable condition, the first members of the Whiteway land group moved in on 29 November 1898. They were Will Sinclair, Owen

Trafford and May and Mac with their babies. The others, as previously stated, used the rented cottages. During the settling-in period, there was a certain amount of reshuffling, for as early as February the following year, Sud had moved over to Whiteway to share a room with Jeannie Straughan in free union, and Jack Bent had also come, to replace Mac who had left, and May who moved to Wishanger with Eiloart.

In that first summer, Whiteway was visited by many people. Some genuine and wondering if this might be the life they could convert to, and some just plain nosey and lazy. They camped out in tents, slept under the stars or if space was made available for them, stayed in Whiteway House. At the onset of separate living, to be looked into in another chapter, Whiteway House once the hub of all communal life, became free for the use of those with genuine needs.

In 1900 Whiteway received some visitors from Russia. Katherine de Kochevskaia, with her sister Sophy, friend Jan, and children Nicholas and Sophie Carmen, had come for refuge to Whiteway on recommendation from Tolstoy himself. Katherine knew him through the teaching of his children, and after her marriage to a banker had broken up, and the birth of Sophie Carmen from another union, it became necessary to swiftly leave Russia without papers or passports, and travel to England for sanctuary.

At Whiteway, the little girl became known as Carmen Maurice, and a detailed account of her time spent here on Whiteway and at school in Sheepscombe is told in a diary which she wrote in about 1914 when she lived in Paris. This account was sent to Sheepscombe by her second husband, Ferdinande Eckhardt, following her death in 1974. It is valuable in its detailed account of what the early days of Whiteway were actually like, as seen through the eyes of a child in a foreign country, who for various reasons, was soon to be left alone.

She writes,

> At the beginning of their new life there, they lived by the rules of Jesus and adoring forth Tolstoi, the great paysant, listening to their conscience and cultivating brother love for one each other. Most ideally minded they wouldn't use any money, just living from earth product, for instance for want of matches, they had to save time and light getting up therefore very early in the morning when the sun rises, and went to bed at sunset time. Lit the fire primitively helping themselves with two bricks and so. We never had bread, and used to eat raw wheat in the hollow of the hand. No salt, no sugar, nothing of this kind. . . .
>
> First we camped together in a big white house situated at the edge of a big white road which had the name Whiteway, and so that house got that name too, 'Whiteway House'.

*A view of Whiteway from the 'sledging field'. Whiteway House is in the centre, flanked on the left by Meadow Cottage and the Photographic Studio, with The Nook behind to the right.*

All people were composed of most interesting personalities. Each of them had visited the university before, or had teached in some high-school, has been or written, polyglot, or at least phylosophe. There were only no artist between them, well maybe there some kind of artist of life, but what I mean, no artist of any beautiful art. . . .

. . . some of them I used to call by their small name . . . there was Nellie Shaw . . . and she has been a darling to me. There was Mr Francis Shollar; he was a man who knew 25 languages, the old ones and those of the present. Then many teachers and architects, all of them having given up their positions and their life which they lived before for the sake of the idea, and became disciples of Tolstoi and Jesus . . .

. . . Small and grown up people were all called by their christian name, for the idea to annoy any family, as were to be all brothers and sisters between them; for instance everyone had the same power on each child, whether it was his own or not.

She recalls how the early Whitewayans were called 'new people' living together with 'no head', and how they thought that Carmen's family must be wealthy as they were the only ones with money there. The hard times of those early years are summed up as follows,

My Aunt Sophy and Nick went once a week to Stroud to hunt for food, as in Whiteway there was entirely nothing, such kinds of things, which they had never had since they abdicated to their normal life to the one they went forth, and I guess when they smelled our cooking, beautiful coffee . . . wonderful Russian soup, roasted meat, they must have felt some way home sic, at least I surpose so. We would have liked to invite all the colonysts to our meals if that would have been possible.

She described the communal way of life, of how trying to live completely together changed during her time here, and they began to build 'their own small cottages'.

Carmen speaks of gathering sticks in the woods twice a week, and carrying water from the 'riverside' in many pails, in preparation for the washing day which was on a Tuesday. Vegetables and fruits were gathered each day, but not so luxurious and delicious as those sent from a shopkeeper friend who spent a holiday at Whiteway with his wife and two daughters. She was not allowed to partake of these.

She explains,

The colonists received also beautiful fruits, oranges, bananas, dates and so on. Friends from London and from other towns came to see us, to see those strange people living so primitively renouncing every luxury, how they did, and this went all around the neighbourhood and people from everywhere came to see us, just by curiosity, and every one who came over spent a gift to us in some wise. Some one brought them a piece of earth so that they could seed more vegetables and fruits, other people sent us a waggon of wood to build a new cottage for a family who seemed to live too much pressed together for want of rooms and so. The Whiteway colonist accepted everything, this, being of Jesus mind about accepting gifts as they said.

When the money which her mother had brought with her began to run out, it was thought advisable that Katherine should return to Russia to earn some more money, while Aunt Sophy stayed behind to care for Nick and Carmen. Very soon she needed to leave also, taking Jan and Carmen's beloved older brother Nick, who needed to continue his academic schooling, with her. Carmen watched sadly as they rode off down the long straight road leaving her all alone in a strange bleak environment.

She was sent to live with Miss Helenn and her two small children, who although on the outset seemed to be suitable, proved otherwise, often

*The road from Miserden to Whiteway. Blue Barn which is just visible was destroyed by fire in the late 1970's.*

*Elfreda and Doreen Protheroe, taken about 1907.*

treating her harshly. When this was discovered, Carmen was removed and placed instead with Jeannie Protheroe, who had two children, Elfreda, then two years old and baby Dorothy. They, it was thought would be company for her. Alas even there she felt alone and unloved without her family.

Now that she was four years old herself and obviously intelligent, it was thought beneficial for her to attend Sheepscombe School with the other Whiteway children, and this she did, walking down daily and enjoying her lessons with the other children there and Kate, the assistant teacher.

The diary says,

> This young lady taught us sometimes in the school. She was the nicest girl to me from all the village. She was a real friend to me and I loved her.

Carmen's natural musical talent was a source of comfort to her in her times of loneliness, and the flowers in the meadow became as alive as people to her, when she composed stories and melodies about them.

She writes,

> That day I heard clearer than ever the music singing in me. It surprised me whistling and singing the melodies imitating some different instruments. Sounds with funny face making sounds. I exactly discerned among them in spite I never heard them realy. . . .
>
> . . . Other days often I used to ask to anyone, 'Listen, don't you hear music?', and I went on humming the melody which was so loud in me that I thought other people must hear it too. To this everyone answered me, 'Imagination!' and went away. No one ever noticed it.

Jeannie who was an accomplished pianist herself, must have recognised this incredible talent for while Carmen was with her she attempted to teach her some pieces on her piano. Carmen writes,

> I played piano on my way. Hardly said, almost unconsciously Jenny taught me some little peaces which I found by myself on the piano while she showed them to me, and helped myself in some clever way. Of course, although she taught me the notes, I did not understand anything of it

When in 1904, Katherine returned to Whiteway to collect Carmen, and she learned of this, she wanted to hear what she could do for herself.

Carmen says,

> Then I began to play (with much help of armings and head noddings) some pieces. Suddenly mother found out I was looking at the music, but my eyes were not following the notes, but went all around, and she kindly asked me to point out, 'Where did I play?'
>
> I was scared! Never I was called to show the place where I was just stopping . . . I turned the page nervously forwards, then backwards, and I could not find the place where she stopped me, then again I found the piece which I played but not the measure, nor less, the note which for my mother took so much interest . . . tears filled my eyes'.

The next day they left to travel to Paris. On the train a nice lady in that apartment passed Carmen a piece of bread and butter with some chicken on it. 'Mother dear, tell her it is an animal.' It looked so appetizing but during her years at Whiteway she had grown up completely vegetarian and so found it impossible to eat. On that train journey as they travelled away from England and Whiteway towards another chapter in her life she recalls, 'Mamy related her long storys about Whiteway and their new people and I fell asleep.'

At the age of ten, Carmen was already studying at the French Conservatoire National, and performing her own compositions before such eminent composers as Ravel and Debussy. In 1920, she married painter Walter Gramatte, and after his death in 1926 married art critic Ferdinande Eckhardt, moving to Canada in 1953, by which time her compositions had become widely acclaimed.

In 1959 she re-visited Whiteway and Sheepscombe, to see those places where the very early years of her life had been spent. The 'little waif' as Jeannie Protheroe had described her, had become a successful, well-known woman.

# *Chapter 5*
# WHITEWAY HOUSE

As the numbers wanting to live in Whiteway House grew, then the same system as that of applying for land for use-occupation was applied.

From about 1906 applications were made through the regularly held meetings, and if several people enquired, then those needing a home more urgently were given preference. A typical example is an extract taken from a letter in January 1913,

> Dear Comrade, Seeing an account of your Colony in the *Daily Herald* of today, it has filled me with a desire to join the same. I am a tailor by trade working in town of which I am thoroughly tired. My wife and I are both out and out socialists and are very anxious to give a good start in life to our little son aged four. My wife is an ex-teacher and we would both be willing to do any work that would be of benefit to the Community. I understand my trade all through and am very fond of the work under good conditions. We are vegetarians and all of us are in good health. We sincerely hope there will be an opportunity for us to join the Commune. Yours fraternally . . .

Alternatively, a portion of another application of February 1919 was likewise received.

> Dear Comrade, Mr Blank whose note I enclose, tells me he is giving up his plot at Whiteway, and is willing to transfer it to me subject to the approval of the resident Colonists. I have been wanting to secure about an acre of land for the last five years, but have not been able to get any with a real security of tenure. As to my eligibility for a place at Whiteway, I can only say that I am a sincere rebel against the conditions of present day society and of the capitalist system upon which it is based. I was for two years Secretary and organiser of the B'ham Federation of BLP branches, and since leaving them for political or rather anti-political reasons, I have developed more towards the anarchist point of view. I maintain that each individual has the natural right of absolute and un-controlled Liberty, so long as he does not interfere with the Freedom and well-being of his fellows. During the war I worked as a gardener and am quite capable of maintaining myself and cultivating the land.
>
> Yours Faithfully . . .

Applications were similarly made for rooms in Whiteway House as depicted below in July 1911.

> Dear Friends, I have heard that the Foster brothers are leaving Whiteway. I should be very glad indeed if you would let me have the part of Whiteway House now occupied by them to live in for a time.
> Yours Faithfully . . .

During the first decade or so, those in occupation in the House were expected to maintain the building if they were able, but when this arrangement proved to be unsatisfactory, and all were worn out with persuading and reminding, then a Whiteway House Repair Fund was introduced, and someone else was paid to do the job.

The garden in which the cottage stood was to be treated in exactly the same way, with portions being granted to those in the cottage if they so wished. When this land proved too small to accommodate all those requiring somewhere to grow themselves some produce, then another piece of land, on which The Nook stands today, was used as well. For those with extra energy, and needing perhaps as much as two acres, then available vacant land elsewhere on colony ground could be applied for and granted, for as long as they used it.

Carmen Maurice and her family were occupying only two rooms in Whiteway House in the year or so that they stayed there, for Hans Jessen, a former member of Purleigh and August Schmidt, a Quaker, used the others.

Schmidt was Swiss and came as early as March 1899, but as to where he lived in those difficult times is not known. What is certain though is that he was one of the first occupants to take a room in Whiteway House when separate living was decided upon. His health was poor for not only did he have a heart complaint, but asthma also. His room was his office, for from it he bought and distributed rare books worldwide, using the postal system for their conveyance.

During the heat of a June day in 1904, he collapsed with a heart attack in his room, and was later discovered there dead. It was the first time a death had occurred on the Colony, so the colonists felt that it would be right and proper to bury him themselves on the land where he had come to seek his freedom. An application to the Council was made and, surprisingly, granted, and after choosing a quiet, beautiful spot at the bottom of Sud's garden, now Panelis, they dug out the grave and laid him to rest in it, wrapped only in a blanket.

Then while Jeannie played Chopin's Funeral March on the piano, he was covered with five inches of soil, and a walnut tree planted on the spot as a memorial.

When it was inspected by the authorities, to see if all had been done correctly, they said it had not been dug deep enough, and Schmidt would have to be dug up and re-interred. No-one wanted to repeat this task, and so two men from the Council had to be sent up to do it instead.

Sud's land was divided in 1920, and Allen put up Panelis, a one-bedroomed hut which grew with his family over the years. Eventually a septic tank was needed. Jack Weston from Sheepscombe was employed to install it, and sent two of his men up to carry out its construction. All was well until they thought they had hit upon Schmidt, and dug up his toe. They refused to carry on, and Jack was sent for to sort the matter out. He cleverly solved the problem by telling them that he was sure that Schmidt would not mind, but the authorities might not like it, so it would be best to move the hole over a bit!

Sam Foster, a teacher, with his brother Fred, a carpenter, mentioned in the letter above, took two rooms in 1909, but were asked to move to the Photographic Studio two years later so that Leah and Matt Kavanagh might live in Whiteway House temporarily, until they could find somewhere more permanent. Shortly afterwards, Sam left the Colony in a caravan,

*William Hodge outside the wash-house.*

wonderfully created by himself and Fred but unfortunately minus a horse with which to draw it. In the end, he had to harness himself to the shafts, and do the 'donkey' work, in order to get it on the road. His brother Fred, after a period during which he married, and went to New Zealand, returned to Whiteway in the twenties, staying at the Long Hut while he built his house, where he lived with his wife Peggie until his death in 1968, making his living as a craftsman in wood.

William Hodge, a retired sailor from St Budeaux in Devon, came in May 1899. His first summer was spent camping out in a tent, though at the onset of winter he thought it sensible to leave, but returned the following spring to live at Bidfield with another Colony member, Ernest Houldy. To prove his intentions of remaining this time, he gave all of sixteen pounds towards the colony expenses. Although not in residence on Whiteway he was still granted some land on which to grow crops, this being the corner piece where Lucifer Lodge stands today.

In 1911 it was decided that a combined weekly contribution should be paid by all those occupying Whiteway House to the value of 30s a year – the very first Whiteway House Repair Fund. Bella Poole was occupying four rooms in the house during this time, with Hale Wortham having just the one, so her contribution was by far the greater, with 24s to find. This probably proved difficult for her, as Bert, her husband followed a nomadic type of existence, tramping around the countryside as the mood took him, and working intermittently on local farms and in the garden of the Stroud Workhouse.

Financial help was therefore irregular and eventually Bella left the Colony with her one child, also called Bella, in 1912. This little girl must have been about five years old, for Leonie Birkenhead can remember her being roughly the same age as herself, a pretty little thing with the most beautiful hair.

Bella's sister Kate lived on Whiteway too at Sainfoin, and was married to Peter Mylles. They lived a more conventional life, completely in contrast to that of Bert and Bella, owning their own home and taking part in Colony affairs.

Three people applied for Bella's share of the rooms. Edwin Rhodes, a cobbler by trade, was the most successful being allotted two of them, while Hale Wortham gained a room by the road with the attic above. It was when Wortham left in 1915, that Hodge was able to come over from Bidfield to use his two rooms.

As Rhodes was in the room which contained the staircase to the attic, it was therefore inconvenient for Hodge to reach his attic room that way, so a vertical ladder was fixed flat onto the wall on the landing between the two rooms, leading to a trap door above. To some this might have proved a somewhat hazardous route, not perhaps to the average person's taste, but this proved no handicap at all to Hodge, who as a sailor was used to shinning up such things.

Although on coming to Whiteway initially Hodge had been generous, donating all he had to the cause, he was not always so, for it was with reluctance that he did odd jobs for Jeannie Protheroe, in exchange for the good meal she kindly gave him every day.

Wortham, while in residence, had looked after the library which was then in the old wash-house, and when he left Hodge took it over. He was a poor librarian though, as he gave books away when he should not have, and got upset when reproved for his way of doing things. Then he would insist that the library was not the colony's property anyway, so therefore they had no say in what he did with it. He maintained it belonged to the Club which had run it when they had used the wash-house as their meeting place, but now that they had disbanded, then he could run it in the way he wished.

To resolve the matter, the remaining Old Club members combined together to sign a petition officially giving it over to the Colony. A few years later it was taken over by Bea Adams and transferred to her house, where her daughter Rene became librarian, and order reigned with the purchase of new books and the introduction of a system of labelling and cataloguing. Hodge however, seemed destined to be connected with the library even in his absence, for when he did eventually leave Whiteway for a sailor's retirement home at Plymouth in 1928, the very room he had occupied in the house was transformed into a library and reading room, which was newly decorated and equipped, with a fund opened to cover the costs of such impressive improvements.

Edwin Rhodes who hailed from Quenyborough in Leicestershire and was known as 'Ned' had an entirely different nature from that of Hodge. When he took over Bella's rooms in Whiteway House, he also applied for and was granted her land at The Nook.

Kathleen Lee from Altringham was allocated half of this ground in 1912, after Rhodes had ensured that his part would remain as land only for cultivation, and Fred Foster was commissioned to build The Nook there, completing it amazingly swiftly by the following December, just six months from its commencement.

When the numbers at Whiteway House decreased and the actual land around it became sufficient for their needs, then Ned's cultivation piece next to the Nook was given up, and was incorporated once more to form the original piece.

In his rooms to the left of the house, Ned repaired the shoes of many of the Colonists. It has been said that after he had mended them, they were better than when newly made. The shoes he made himself were a work of art and there is little doubt that he was a true master at his craft.

*The Nook.*

Whiteway children were always welcome to visit whoever they pleased on the Colony and would go to see one and another as they felt. Whereas Hodge was rarely honoured with their company, with Ned it was a different story altogether. They knew that he did not mind them sitting and talking to him as he worked.

Once when Rene Adams was about eight years old and Ned was the one chosen to be favoured with a visit from her that day, she asked him to make a pair of shoes for her best doll, whom she loved. He produced the most exquisite miniature shoes ever seen and Rene was delighted and the envy of all her friends. The only problem was that Rene's mother, Bea had not known about it and when she received a bill for 5s she was aghast, and said she could not afford it. So Ned did the only thing he could do, and that was to give them to her.

His generosity was not so freely given when a Muslim called Alfred Ashton arrived on Whiteway with a young woman, parking his old caravan on the Old Playground land above Whiteway House. When Ashton made it known that he would like to have use of the wash-house which Ned considered his domain at that time, there was an argument and fight, resulting in Ned backing down, and Ashton taking it over.

Ashton did not mix with the other Colonists much, but when he did, trouble usually resulted. He was unfortunate to be endowed with a sensitive disposition, being inclined to quarrel. In 1921 after a disagreement with George Allen, a man himself immoveable in his convictions, Ashton set fire to George's shed in the middle of the night, with damage to the value of £50 resulting. After that his reputation as a fire worshipper grew, and no one felt safe any more, so it was agreed that it would be better if he left.

There were plenty of strong men available on that day to assist him on his way, and between them they moved his caravan along the road to Birdlip Woods until they thought that a suitable and safe distance had been covered between him and the Colony.

Edwin Rhodes suffered a stroke in 1926, and following a stay in Stroud Hospital, he went to live with his daughter in Manchester. It was necessary to know what to do concerning his rooms in the house, and so a letter was sent to his daughter asking her what her father intended to do about them but no-one replied. He had, before he left, sold his small amount of furniture to Alice Woore, a woman of gypsy-like appearance, but who apparently came from good stock. In fact anyone who doubted this, instantly changed their minds when she opened her mouth to speak, for the voice that emerged was so cultured that any disbelief was immediately dispelled. She lived in a shack on Clay Piece, where she kept a few chickens and a cow.

This cow would be brought to the Old Children's Playground each evening for milking, and colonists would buy milk, together with the butter and cream which she made, from her.

On Ned's departure she thought that she would like to live in the rooms vacated by him, and duly applied for them. Two others applied also. One was Edwin Coles who having no where else to go was living in the Stroud Workhouse and the other was Ethel Portlock who with her youngest son Charlie was in Will Cole's shed at Burnt Piece.

As Alice already had a home of her own and some thought that her wish to get into the cottage might not be in the best interests of the Colony, it was decided that preference should go to Ethel and Will, with Ethel getting two of Ned's rooms and Will one. Alice however insisted that she was there in order to look after Rhodes' rooms and property and so must remain there until he returned.

Another letter was written to Ned, asking if indeed he was intending to return, but still with no response, until finally a letter was sent by registered post. In it, he was asked to remove his belongings within ten days, or they would be taken out and stored in the wash-house.

When the stated time was up, and there was still no news, five colonists went to clear the rooms, so that Ethel could use them. On finding them locked, they had no alternative but to break in, an action alien to Whiteway

*Pat Smiddy, basket maker.*

principles, and remove the contents there for storage in the wash-house as promised. Ethel was then able to move into her rooms.

Two days later at eleven o'clock at night, when Ethel was in bed, Alice with two friends to support her, turned up, with the result that Ethel and all her belongings were pushed out of the window. Hodge who was in his room heard all the noise, and went post haste up to the Hall to where colonists were attending a dance. Most of the dancers then poured down the road to the house, and after an hour or more of arguing and persuading, finally evicted Alice, and reinstated Ethel. For the remainder of the week a watch was kept so ensuring that now Alice was out, she would stay out.

Solicitors' letters were exchanged when Alice complained that the items that she acquired from Rhodes were locked away from her, and she was not allowed to get them. After a full and explanatory letter to her solicitor from Sinclair, explaining the ownership and room allocation system, the key was produced and Alice collected the things which she claimed were hers.

Ethel Portlock now secure in Whiteway House was poor and went charring for 6d an hour. Although her job was lowly and poorly paid, she did remarkably well from it in one way or another, for all who employed her rewarded her efforts with an assortment of extras, so much so, that it was not too long before her rooms were furnished with all that she needed.

She married Pat Smiddy, an Irishman from Liverpool, who after moving to the Stroud area lived at Cranham where he worked as a forester with Jim Allen at Annis. He was due to marry Ethel in the Registry Office on St Patrick's Day, but the night before Pat got so drunk that the ceremony had to be called off, and was held the following week.

Misfortune clouded Pat's life, for during his forestry days he had a bad accident in which he was hit on the shoulder by an axe and then gradually, over a period of time, he began to lose his sight, eventually having to have an eye removed, and a glass one put in to replace it. By 1946 he was almost totally blind. He was obliged to give up his forestry work, and with the help of the National Institute of the Blind, a workshop was erected on the site of the old wash-house, where he carried on basketry work to bring in a wage. Later, the same consultant who helped to improve Leonie Blackwood's eyesight, restored the sight in his other eye, so that he could now see his way up the road to the pub a mile away.

By 1944 Pat and Ethel had taken over the entire house. Ethel's crippled sister moved in with her then, living in the sitting room overlooking the road, and staying until she died. Bit by bit as rooms became free, they acquired another room, and from that time forth Whiteway House was never used by more than one family at a time.

Many had lived there since the time of Hodge and Rhodes. There was Ernest Adams who when it was decided to get rid of an old caravan on the Children's Playground into which he had settled, was offered one of the rooms left free when Alice Woore was persuaded to leave. Lilian Wolfe and another colonist Charlie Keene contributed a bed and other necessities for him, but a year later he too, was required to leave on his refusal to pay his contribution of five shillings towards the rates.

On his departure, Luke took over his room for six months, and Noel got the room above the library room for 1s a week.

When it ceased to be used as a circulating library, due to general lack of interest, even though lists of available books were posted up in the Hall for all to see, it became Walter and Elfie Clark's cobblers shop, which they initially took for one year but used for three.

When it was realised that Noel and Walter were using their rooms infrequently, and an old friend from Whiteway's very early days needed a home, they returned their keys and Whiteway was able to repay Adolph Abrahams and his daughter for all the generosity he had shown to them during those difficult pioneering times, just because they had been able to stay a few weeks on the Colony now and again.

In 1939, five Spanish refugees were able to use the two rooms near the road, although not all at once, and on their departure, Heluth, another refugee and a couple from Vienna came.

In 1942 when it was seen that Ethel and Pat had gained use of the entire house, as room by room became vacant, some colonists complained. They felt that it was not in the proper Whiteway tradition, and that it should be treated as a refuge for those in need as before. Others pointed out that Ethel's need was as great as anyones, so the situation remained as it stood. The repair fund money was increased to fifteen shillings a week though, and there were always plenty of repairs to spend it on.

Whiteway House acquired its water supply in 1948, with the rest of the Colony, and its electric current in 1955, but eventually time and exhaustion took over, and in 1973 it became empty for the first time for seventy-five years, and remained so during the seven years it took to carry out necessary repairs.

# *Chapter 6*
# THE WASH-HOUSE AND STUDIO

Any plans concerning development on the new farm project were automatically shelved when the anticipated amount of money was reduced so dramatically. Only enough was available for a variety of fruit trees and seeds to sow for the harvest ahead.

Short of money they might have been but short of stone they definitely were not. There was always difficulty with the washing, and as Whiteway House was bursting at the seams with Colonists and visitors, there was a need for somewhere to undertake this tiresome but necessary chore, which hitherto had been done outside.

Digging began in 1898 near the corner of the Wet Ground field, as it soon became known for obvious reasons, and enough stone was quarried during the first summer to build an out-house at the top of the Whiteway House garden.

During its life its uses were many, until it was eventually demolished in 1933. For its first ten years all washing was done there, either collectively or later individually as required. It contained all the necessary equipment for its purpose. Those using these items were expected to leave them in a fit state for the colonist who needed them another time. But this was not always adhered to, and the wringer was left uncleaned and began to fall into a poor state of repair. It was removed to Nellie Shaw's, where whoever required it, had to go to the trouble of fetching it and subsequently returning it satisfactorily cleaned afterwards.

In later years as Colonists settled into their own homes and therefore had more space available, washing began to be done at home, with water collected from their roofs in water butts or by making several journeys with containers, taking the shortest possible route to the stream at the bottom of Fred Foster's garden.

After about a decade of Colonists fetching wood, stoking up the copper, and prodding down the washing, the wash-house became a Colony store, where groceries could be bought reasonably when ordered through the storeman. The opening hours were limited from seven to eight in the evening at its commencement, but increased substantially as time progressed, until they stretched from ten in the morning to four in the afternoon.

Sam Foster was storeman at the time when there were complaints over the fluctuation of opening times, and that some of the groceries were being bought directly by individuals, instead of through the store as arranged. There was moaning and groaning over the quality and prices of goods, together with accusations of mice droppings and lentils in with the sugar and rice. After a meeting in which the whole issue was discussed at length, Sinclair was asked to take care of the situation, with stock taking, investigating suppliers, finding the source of an unpleasant smell and mousetraps.

In October, when Sam's year was up, Leah Kavanagh took over the job, and for payment of about five shillings a week, ran the store in a more orderly fashion. As happens with any enterprise, even one undertaken with a willing spirit, things rarely run smoothly. Having got the hours and suppliers sorted out, Leah then announced that there had been some pilfering of the lump sugar and oatmeal, and unhappily this resulted in a padlock being put on the wash house door. The stores did not remain much longer in their mice-ridden barricaded home however, for in the following January, a leak had developed in the roof, and all the goods were transferred to the safer and drier passageway of the home of Colony Secretary, Peter Mylles, at Sainfoin. With this transfer came enlargement.

George Mackenzie, a Scotsman renowned for his countless marvellous plans for the development of Whiteway suggested that the store and Colonists could all benefit if the store opened wholesale accounts with firms supplying more varied and larger items. The products would be delivered to colonists' doors, with no fuss, and still include a five per cent discount on monthly accounts. This resulted in bill heads being printed, and accounts opened with a wholesale newspaper agent, the Gloucester Iron and Hardwear Co, and JB Fleet, a clock and jewellery repairer. The only stipulation to this plan was that all goods supplied had to be paid for in cash. There was no credit.

Newspapers were to be supplied weekly, at no extra cost even though they came to the back of beyond, and if a letter was produced from the storekeeper to Mr Webb, the Lewis and Godfrey's secretary in Stroud, then a variety of goods from clothes to bedding was available, all very reasonably priced.

Coal could be ordered, with delivery ensured if the weather was not too bad, and those who wished for artificial manure, instead of the good strong real stuff from up the road, could get that too.

A list of goods always in stock recorded at the time is as follows: stationary: writing paper, envelopes and blotting paper; Ambassador, Waverley and Relief pens; black lead and copying pencils; Stephen's blue-black ink; 1d packets of luggage tags; haberdashery: pins, needles, thimbles and hairpins; linen, pearl, shirt, trouser and boot buttons, also plaquet closers, black and white; elastic tapes; cotton and linen thread, darning wools; also lamp wicks, three quarter and an inch. Anything in fact, could be purchased from anywhere in the United Kingdom, at very reasonable prices, when ordered through the Store.

In April 1911, Leah resigned as storekeeper and left the Colony. She had run it profitably, with no outstanding debts, and for her efforts much gratitude was expressed.

She was replaced by Peter Mylles and his wife Kate, who ran the entire enterprise from their home. This would seem to have been the most sensible arrangement anyway, as the main part of the stock was already there. Peter did his utmost to make the store a success. He shopped for practically all the Whiteway households, endeavouring to supply any item requested, transporting it himself if it was possible. But for all his efforts, there was always someone he could not please. There were always complaints of inferior quality, it was not the right type, or it cost too much. Eventually fed up with the pressure and trouble of it all, he decided to pack it in.

George Mackenzie took the store on, with the sure confidence which he always had, of resurrecting its popularity, and increasing the profit margin.

As Peter Mylles had secured employment elsewhere and needed to leave Whiteway, he had sold his house to William Wexham, and so another home was needed for the stores. This was solved temporarily when Will agreed that his shed could be used for storage for another three months, after which he would like the stock to be removed.

George promised the meeting that by the end of the year he would be able to submit a report as to the state of the store, its falling sales and now gathering debts, when he was certain that improvements regarding both would have been remedied. Unfortunately for poor George, when January came and it was time for his report, the situation had become so bad that it was agreed by all that it would be impossible for the store to continue, and something should be done.

It was run as the Colony Store for just one more week, and then on the last day of the month, it was handed over to Will Wexham to be run as a private concern from a shop extension, now the kitchen, added to his house. From here he supplied other villages too, and this particular shop was never run as a communal venture again.

Will paid £14 for it, with £7 being paid there and then, and the remaining £7 six months later.

He too failed to get it on its feet, for the Colonists ceased to use it when Sud Protheroe began his shop at his bakery a few years later.

With the wash house now vacant, time was ripe for another brainwave scheme thought up by George. This time it was a Colony Club Room. All

*The Photographic Studio, the only building brought to Whiteway during the first year.*

was considered, involving the cost of repairing the roof and any conversion in general. It was estimated that £4 would see to the roof, the replacing of broken tiles, the boarding inside and the plastering of the walls. Mackenzie assisted by three other Colonists embarked on these repairs, but it was not until the end of 1912 that the wash house, now changed into the Whiteway Club Room, was ready to welcome its members.

By 1916, when the Club had ceased to exist and the library created by them had been moved out, the wash house was used for a variety of purposes. The Bakery used it until 1930, Rene had it as a workshop, someone else was thinking of converting it into a garage, and all and sundry used it to store things in.

Finally in April 1933, it was pulled down and the stone divided between Will Cole to repair the wall by Whiteway House and the Sports Group who were building a tennis court. Thirty-three years of activity reduced to a pile of rubble in just six months.

The only other type of shelter available to the new settlers during that first year of 1898, was a corrugated tin hut. This was really a photographic studio which was acquired and placed in the same corner of the field as the quarry. When Jeannie and Sud needed a place to themselves away from the crush in Whiteway House, it was pulled down and re-erected on the land just below Whiteway House.

It was on this piece of ground that Sud chose to build his own home,

*Sketch by Gassy showing the arrangement of the three first Whiteway buildings. The wash-house on the left, Whiteway House in the centre, with The Photographic Studio situated below in the meadow, on the site it occupies today.*

Meadow Cottage. He built it only a few yards away from the Studio, so close in fact that today the two parts are fused together to form one dwelling. Most probably he had begun to cultivate the land while living in the Studio, and thought it wise to remain on the same land, and benefit from all the effort he had put into it.

When his newly built house was completed, Sud and Jeannie moved across the gap to it, and The Studio was used as short term accommodation for single people and those with families temporarily until they had built their own home or found accommodation elsewhere.

We know little of it after 1912, but we do know that the Boynton family stayed there for quite a long time while their son Dennis was building them a house on the non-Whiteway land further up the road, and the Kavanaghs and the Foster brothers occupied it briefly.

After 1930 it came once more into the hands of the Protheroe family, and was occupied by them with a covered way eventually joining it to the main house.

# Chapter 7

# THE MOVE TO INDIVIDUAL LIVING

We have talked of Whiteway House which was communally held, and seen how it was the centre of all activity during the first two years of the Colony's life. It had become obvious as time progressed that living as a combined unit would not be possible for any long term plan, so some aspects of colonists' lifestyle would need to change.

Those determined members still remaining on Whiteway felt a need to spread themselves, some had united into pairs, and some singles occasionally felt the need for solitude. So a decision was made, after much heart searching, that individual accommodation should be adopted within the continuing framework of communal living.

The four remaining original settlers, Sinclair, Nellie, Sud and Jeannie, each chose a piece of land on the Wet Ground, large enough for their needs and near to water. Sud and Jeannie having been united in a free union relationship for nearly two years already, and living in the Studio, seemed to

*Sinclair in the doorway of his thatched hut. The row of trees on the horizon is still there, as a clue to where it stood.*

be the two most immediately in need. So Sinclair, assisted by Sud, began to make bricks as he had learned to at Purleigh.

Clay had been found by the stream, and this was extracted, moulded and baked until an appropriate number had been manufactured. Having been inconsistently fired, the standard was poor, and those suitable were limited in number, so any idea of constructing a family home, however modest was out of the question. So Sinclair kept them, and used them instead for his own small hut, placed well away to the left hand corner of the Wet Ground in four acres of land. It cost nothing but the effort of building it, for Farmer Causey contributed the straw for the thatched roof, and its bunk bed arrangement inside was simple but adequate.

Sud's house on the other hand was larger, built of wood and paid for by his family. He built it in the pretty little paddock below Whiteway House known as 'Little Meadow', up against his boundary which ran alongside the track that went through to Miserden. One door opened straight onto the road, and the other into his garden. A verandah along its front contributed towards it being a very attractive house.

The accommodation consisted of two bedrooms and a sitting room, with a kitchen and a bathroom overlooking the road. The bathroom was

*Meadow Cottage newly built in 1902.*

*The Protheroe family on the verandah at Meadow Cottage. Sud is on the left with Jeannie in the centre.*

*Elfie and Dods. Difficult to tell apart.*

equipped with three baths of varying sizes with a copper for the hot water to fill them with, but no toilet. All toilets in those days were sited in the proper place, in the garden! Theirs was up a steep path. Jennifer recalls how this was easy to run to at the last minute in summer, but slippery and liable to involve an accident of one kind or another if rushing when the ice was on the ground.

The nicest room was the spacious sitting room with its large bay window. It was used from the moment it was built for every kind of meeting, from those solemn ones connected with colony matters, to the social ones, Jeannie's musical evenings and Children's Party. This was organised by Jeannie for many years, in addition to the usual Colony one on Boxing Day and was looked forward to with anticipation. The most memorable part, and the one that all the children waited for, was Jeannie's Bran Tub, the mysterious contents of which were chosen and wrapped by Jeannie herself, ready for those eager hands to rummage for and discover.

Sud and Jeannie's first daughter Elfreda, or 'Elfie,' was born in the Studio in 1902, their own house not being completed sufficiently to receive a new baby. Dorothy, or 'Dods' as she was always known, fared better, for in 1904 when she entered this world, all was shipshape and in good repair.

As young children they slept in the attic, which had a small skylight, and was reached by a ladder from the sitting room. However as they grew, this sleeping arrangement had to be abandoned, for the only place where it was possible to stand up straight was in the middle of the room, so it became from then on, a place to store vegetables and fruit instead.

Today the small skylight is no more, being dispensed with when a brand new red roof was put on in 1991.

When Elfie had her own family of three children, Lyn, John and Jennifer, they all lived in the Studio, until Jeannie died and they took over the family home. It was divided to contain two bedrooms and a sitting room, in which Elfie did all her cooking over oil stoves which had three burners.

Today Meadow Cottage is much enlarged to its right, but the part constructed by Sud still looks the same as it did when newly built.

The same year as Meadow Cottage and Sinclair's Hut were built, Nellie Shaw and Francis Sedlak built their home. Francis had joined during the difficult months of that first summer when all had been unsettled with Sam and the land situation. None of this had deterred him from staying, for his own life had been a continuous sequence of traumatic events, and this one at Whiteway doubtless seemed small by comparison. After working his passage from his native Bohemia through the French Foreign Legion in Algiers, he overcame imprisonment by escaping into the Sahara desert, only to be further imprisoned in Spain. After release on payment of a fine and despised

*Sunnymedes, Nellie Shaw's house.*

miliary service in his country, he visited England and Russia where he met Tolstoy who advised him about Purleigh which upon his arrival there was practically no more with only the Hones in residence.

Whiteway beckoned and so he came, arriving at Stroud in the evening, and after walking up the Slad to Bulls Cross he fell asleep until the morning when after breakfast with the Brachers at Sheepscombe, he arrived at Whiteway where he remained until his death.

Being a philosopher, he wrote a book entitled *Pure Thought and the Riddle of the Universe*. In a quote from *The Stroud News* he claimed in a sentence 'to have solved once and for all the constitution of the cosmos by the practical application of Hegel's laws of pure thought.' His formulae were calculated by the distance of the earth from the sun, the diameter of the moon, the length of Neptune's day, or any other astronomical measurement can be ascertained to within a fraction of a mile, or of a second without the aid of a single experimental observation. To master the art of pure thinking was the answer to all metaphysical problems, for through it, perfect self knowledge could be achieved and barriers removed.

Before her involvement with Francis, Nellie had been living at Climperwell with firstly her friend Lucy, and then her mother, an

*Francis Sedlak. During the no-money period, and feeling unable to use the government-backed postal system, Francis attempted to walk to London to deliver the second part of his article 'My Military Experiences' to the New Order Office. The weather was very cold with heavy snow and he was clad only in thin clothes with no shoes. Not surprisingly he was forced to turn back following an uncomfortable night in a publican's barn at Barnsley.*

unsatisfactory arrangement for everyone when her relationship with Francis developed, and they needed to be on their own.

In her book, *A Colony on the Cotswolds*, published in 1935, she relates how Arthur St John, a friend from the Croydon Brotherhood days, sent her forty pounds just at the right time, to build herself a house. It cost thirty-seven pounds and ten shillings, including transportation from Gloucester, with still enough left to spend on fruit and nut trees.

Francis built the house himself, a magnificent accomplishment for one who is happier dealing with matters concerning the mind. The land they chose was further down Little Meadow near the stream, adjoining Sud's land.

The house remains today virtually as it was when newly built, the kitchen roof has been raised and perhaps a few minor items have been altered but on the whole Nellie would have been pleased, for she did not want it changed.

To supplement her income Nellie took in visitors, as did many of the other colonists. The people who swarmed to Whiteway on its formation did decrease in number, but there were always enough people wanting to stay for a holiday on Whiteway to keep everyone satisfied for a good many years, by which time only one or two colonists were taking them in, Nellie being one of them.

In 1944, Nellie celebrated her eightieth birthday, and a party was held for her in Whiteway Hall, with Ted Adams, one of the older Colonists from

1906, presenting her with a cheque for eight guineas from all her friends on the Colony. Two years later, she became ill, and on 17 December, after a stay of two weeks at Resthaven Nursing Home, she died. Her funeral was simple, but Nellie would have liked it. Mr Parker, who farmed Hilltop Farm, loaned his cart which was covered with straw and duly decorated. It was used to carry her on her last journey to Miserden that Thursday morning in style, where she was buried in the Whiteway Corner, an unconsecrated part of Miserden Churchyard, next to her beloved Francis.

With individual properties came expense. Having dispensed with the initial building costs, there was still maintenance, furnishing, and rates. There was always trouble with the rates even when members were living communally.

During the first year, when the no-money phase was in operation, and only a few colonists were still indulging in the usual form of currency Joe Burtt, who understandably had been unable to dispense with what previously had constituted his livelihood, saved the day by paying the rates himself.

The second year, as he was no longer around, and even those who still used money had none, Jeannie's precious piano was taken. It was kept for over twelve months before her brother Will retrieved it for her, at the cost of £3 5s 2d, including storage.

Walter Wentworth, Sud and Arnold Eiloart all went to prison during those years as a result of their feelings on this enforced commitment. But it soon became apparent that the rates and the tithe, a subject indulged upon later, were a necessary evil, and by 1910, the money for them was being raised in one way or another.

It was obvious though that money was now needed, and Sud and Sinclair began, each in a small way, to earn some. The bread making learned during Sud's Purleigh days, now proved to be beneficial. He was already producing bread for his own family, and some friends, which was proving extremely popular and now, with the addition of a brick built oven, he increased his output to cater for those from elsewhere.

After baking on the Friday night, he walked down to Sheepscombe on the Saturday morning, where the bread was swiftly sold to an increasing number of appreciative customers. This was the small beginning of a business which was to grow in popularity throughout the British Isles.

Sinclair's way of life changed more dramatically. He had been sharing his hut with Walter Wentworth, a former student from Ruskin College, Oxford since the time he had assisted in it's building, and although it was small it had been adequate for their needs, both being single men.

Everything changed when Mary Kelly and her sister Rachelle Edelman, both Russian Jews from New Jersey, visited Whiteway in 1904. They became acquainted with Sinclair and Walter when Rachelle asked permission to graze her two cows on his land. From there, a friendship developed and grew between them all, and shortly Mary and Walter embarked on a free union relationship. This resulted in Walter moving out of the hut, and building a bungalow further across the Wet Ground for himself, Mary and baby Walter to live in. This house he called Woodcot, and they lived there for six years, until they emigrated to another colony in Oregon in 1910.

Cautious Sinclair was not quite so hasty, for it was another two years before he threw off his forty-three years as a bachelor and set up home with Rachelle, and her two children, John and Sonia, in the new farmhouse he had built. During the time of its building, he had stayed with his friends, Charlie Keene and Charles Stewart, in Sheepscombe in one of the Yew Tree cottages, moving back to Whiteway on completion of the house in 1906.

The new house, Bidwell, named after the stream which ran nearby, was substantially larger and stronger than his former abode, eventually becoming two storied and constructed with brick. This house not only boasted a large front room, but a parlour and kitchenette as well, together with another extra downstairs room, suitable for any occasion. Upstairs there were three bedrooms and a bathroom, which was fitted with an Elsan and water on tap – if the tank had been filled by some energetic person operating the pump from below in the kitchen. Along the length of its frontage ran a

*Bidwell, Sinclair's farmhouse. The lower storey is rendered, and the top storey is built of wood added later possibly by Fred Foster. The roof style is certainly similar to others he built on Whiteway.*

*Joy Robert fetching the milk from Sinclair's farm.*

verandah, and the roof was of the hipped variety, which allowed more space upstairs.

No-one knows exactly what happened to his old hut. It may have been incorporated into his cow shed, which in turn reverted to a basic form of dwelling in 1929, with a complete conversion in 1940.

Their dairy business began simply, with the colonists purchasing any milk they had, but as the two cows increased to three and then to five, Sinclair began supplying those in other villages, not only with his milk, but with butter and cheeses made by Rachelle, which she hung to drip in a row along the verandah in bags, until they were ready. They could be seen in those days from right along the track, an impossibility today, as there are so many trees. They also took in paying guests who, in turn also, bought their dairy produce.

When the Small Holdings Act came into force in 1913, Sinclair was able to lease two extra fields from Miserden Estate, so increasing his land by an extra ten acres, a necessity in the summer when the Colony was invaded by an influx of visitors. In fact the demand for dairy products became so great that in 1926 he entered into partnership with George Kenworthy, who ran a carrier's business from his premises at Hilltop Farm and, with the added twenty-six acres of pasture land that this transaction brought about, more cows were purchased bringing the number up to twelve. Sinclair's customers were now around the hundred mark, and it is fair to say that the dairy had proved itself successful.

Then it became known that Rachelle and Sinclair were thinking of selling up and moving to America to be with their children who had settled there. Sinclair's heart was at Whiteway, and it has been said that he really did not want to go. As it turned out he never left Whiteway for in 1928 he suffered a fall and sustained head injuries from which he never recovered.

After his death Rachelle stayed on for another eighteen months or so, but eventually decided to join her children at the Stelton Colony in New Jersey in December 1929.

Maisie and Sidney Hall came from Cardiff and farmed Bidwell in the old tradition for about six years after that, but when they split up, Maisie sold the farmhouse and moved up to live in her cow shed with her daughter Trixie. The farm which Sinclair had begun thirty years before, was divided up for new settlers, so closing the chapter of thirty years of farming on Colony land.

# *Chapter 8*

# PROTHEROE'S BAKERY

Sudbury Protheroe's Bakery became important to the whole community, for many of its population were at one time or another employed there. In its infancy, Jeannie helped Sud, but as it grew help from outside the family was needed.

By 1906 there was a need for premises away from the house, where there would be more space to cater for this increase. This problem was solved when Sud's brother Alec decided to leave the Colony. His partly built bungalow, situated near the site of the former Photographic Studio, was pulled down by Sud and Walter Wentworth, and re-erected on the top of the slope above Meadow Cottage.

Sud's brick oven was replaced by another portable one, to be changed yet again as his enterprise further expanded to a double oven, with each oven having the capacity to hold 110 loaves. This remains in the Bakery today.

Sud's bread was called Old English, and was made from stoneground flour, ground locally at Edgeworth Mill, just a few miles away. With the addition

*The Protheroe Bakery.*

*Working in the Bakehouse during the 1914–18 war. Note the bare feet.*

of the best quality ingredients, which Sud insisted on using even when the War was on and things were scarce, he produced a delicious loaf.

Alice Birkenhead was his first assistant from outside his family. She lived at Woodcot, Walter Wentworth's house, and worked for Sud for several years. Other helpers began to be employed. When an outlet became available at Miss Eamonson's Health Food Store in Clarence Street, Cheltenham, he was obliged to change his baking day from Friday to Sunday, so that deliveries could be made to the shop early on Monday morning.

His delivery method, once done in a leisurely way on foot and by bicycle, now changed to West's carrier cart of Sheepscombe. West though, for a reason best known to himself, could rarely be tempted to venture into Whiteway, so all goods had to be taken up to the Fostons Ash pub, from where they were collected. It must have been a relief therefore when George and Fred Kenworthy took over this task instead, for as their stables were already at Whiteway, and they lived here also, the bread could be loaded up straight from the bakery door and distributed without further trouble. Towards the end of the First World War, Sud had progressed even further to being the proud owner of a Model T Ford van.

His bread products had become so popular, that other bakers in Cheltenham and the surrounding area became concerned that their livelihoods would suffer. They need not have worried however, for with

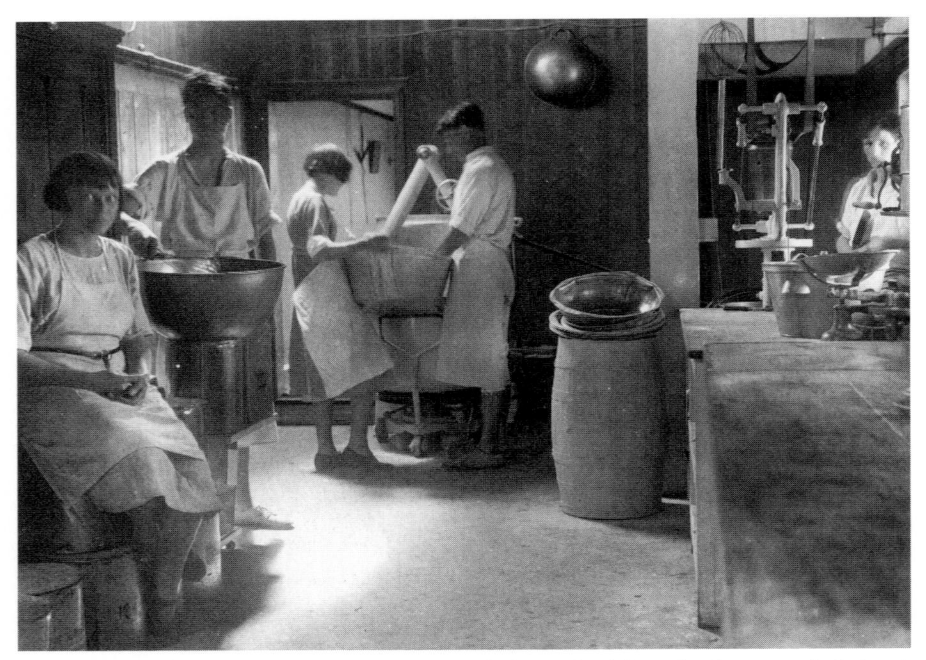

*Another wartime photograph. Elfie assists Sud in the background, while Dods takes a rest. Sud's bread was in demand so much during the war that it was impossible to supply everyone who required it.*

petrol rationing being introduced, Sud's journeys were reduced accordingly, and often he could only manage a trip once a week.

With an eye to distribution further afield, he began to bake cakes, so making a larger variety of products available to the customer. The most popular was from a recipe of his mothers called Rizza cake. Shortbread and biscuits, and a variety of cakes and tarts were all produced in addition to his normal breads, and consequently Sud was obliged to work virtually day and night to get the orders out.

He was now supplying schools, shops and hotels, some as far away as Salisbury and Weston Super Mare. Belfast and Scotland were also covered, with mainly shortcake going to the latter. Some of his cakes were even exported all over the world in special hermetically sealed tins.

In about 1920 there was a change in Sud's personal and business life. He moved out of Meadow Cottage, and built himself a bed-sit complete with fireplace and a space under the floor to keep his fats cool, onto the left side of the Bakehouse.

When, a couple of years later, he inherited some money, he employed a local building firm, Freemans of Camp, to build him another house just a few yards from his bakery. This was more commodious than his first home

*Sud, with Dorothy to the left.*

of Meadow Cottage, being two storied and constructed of stone. Its upper half was clad in barge boarding, and its windows were diamond leaded. Here he lived for the next ten years with his second wife Dorothy MacDougal, a former medical student he had met while she was staying at Jeannie's on holiday. They had three children of their own, Jacky, Jane known as Tupps and a son Ian.

His bed-sit then became a shop, beginning humbly with basic commodities such as flours and sugars, until eventually it was stocking all manner of goods and vegetables. Now that Will Wexham's store was no more, Sud's shop became popular, being open all day and selling his bakery products as well. Sud's two daughters Elfie and Dods were now grown up, and both involved in the business. Dods worked in the shop, and Elfie was involved with the packing.

Lambert Smith, from Wishanger, having been discharged from the army, was employed in deliveries. In 1923 he bought himself a piece of land on the non-Whiteway ground, and built a bungalow there, near the Boynton's house, where he lived with his first wife Lilian and baby Brian. He was also proud to be the driver of Sud's new delivery vehicle which was a converted 21 hp Chrysler car, onto which a 15 cwt van body had been constructed. With this powerful machine Lambert was able to cover about eight hundred miles a week, supplying bread and cakes to customers near and far.

*Sud with his second family outside Halstead in 1929.*

He usually finished at Leckhampton Railway Station, where after collecting any waiting materials, he drove back to Whiteway. After cleaning his van ready for the next day's load, his working day was finished.

Austin Jones and Reginald Short, Elfie's and Dods' husbands, respectively, both worked at the bakery. Reginald particularly had a good business head, and during this period everything was thriving.

Because of this happy situation the bakery entered into a co-operative scheme, in which all the employees became partners and all were paid the same.

Sud was now able to devote his energies more to another interest he was developing, that of confectionary. He erected a hut near the bakery for this purpose, and within four years was hardly involved with the bakery at all, leaving its running to the Co-operative. The jams and fudges that he produced were exquisite, all being beautifully wrapped. Sud took as much trouble with them as he had done with his breads, and it paid off, for he was able to sell his products to best quality shops.

The blow came in May 1926 with the General Strike.

All the orders and deliveries to the Bakery which normally travelled by train, now had to stay at home. The resulting drop in income, on which so

*Sud with baby Jacqueline, Dods and her husband Reginald Short, at The Cloisters in 1927.*

many were reliant, plus the steady decline in the country generally throughout the next few years, caused much concern. The Co-operative scheme finally broke up after about five years, hastened on when Sud withdrew completely in order to be totally involved with his new enterprise.

Lambert's marriage to Lilian was also in difficulties and they too parted.

Lambert now took on the resonsibility of the ailing Bakery, and for the next eleven years he ran both the baking and sales side under considerable financial pressure.

The bakery was still in a precarious situation in 1935 when Sud made the decision to broaden his horizons and buy a shop in Salisbury, and here he produced and sold his exclusive confectionary and wholefood products until his death in 1955.

Miss Eamonson, the bakery's long time customer and friend from its early days bought Protheroe's Bakery in those troublesome times, so saving it from bankruptcy, even though she had only recently acquired the Oxford Health Food Stores, and probably did not need another shop at that time.

She changed little in its running only to the extent of removing all meat products from the shelves, the shop from then on being entirely vegetarian. As she was not intending to live on Whiteway and so did not require Sud's house Lambert as the manager took up residence there letting his own house of Meadoways to Harry and Ivy Merrett, bakers at Protheroe's for many years.

*The Bakery ovens. L–R: Mary Workman, Harold Merrett and Lottice Davies. Mary worked in the bakery until forced to retire by illness, from which she died in 1973. With her husband Les she came from Sheepscombe in 1940 to settle on Whiteway. They sited the cabin they brought with them on the Dry Ground in George Barker's chicken run, in the same spot originally occupied by The Croft. Les was a well-known bee-keeper and the Bee-Keeper's Field Day was held at Whiteway for many years during his lifetime. His mead and honey cakes were widely acclaimed, as were Mary's jumble sales from which nothing was allowed to be sold before the doors opened.*

In 1948 Lambert left Whiteway and began the Gloucester Health Food Shop with his second wife Andree. The bakery business was sold to Patrick Elliott,who ran it and drove the delivery van, assisted by Alec Barber from Stroud. In April 1953 Doris Gilmore, who had only moved into The Bungalow three weeks before, began working in the office. There were also Muriel and Gerald Phelps, Muriel being Harry and Ivy's daughter, with Mary Workman, involved with the decorating and packaging side, and Leonie Blackwood with Dora Price, Muriel's sister, serving in the shop. Maureen Light, granddaughter of Polly and Will Light, early settlers from 1922, came to work her skills on the cake decoration and Lottice Davies together with Ivy and Harold worked in the Bakery.

*The Protheroe delivery van with Elfie's son Lyn.*

Pat Elliott ran the bakery until 1967 when he asked Colin Price, who was in charge of the Miserden Shop and a grocery business, if he would like to take over the bakery with it's practical work, while he continued with the administrative side. Consequently, on Pat's retirement Colin became the Bakery's new owner.

Protheroe's was still sending its products some distance – to Torquay, Edinburgh, Belfast and Dundee by rail. This had to cease when the costing system changed to that of mileage and weight instead of per box, thus proving uneconomical. Colin took care of Protheroe's Bakery and Shop for twenty years without major mishap until, in 1989, something occurred which changed everything.

Annual checks had always been carried out on the Bakery equipment to ensure that all was safe and working. As usual it received such treatment in January 1989, and was declared fit. On 9 March that year, there was an explosion, due, it was thought, to a weak tube in the oven. When the oven was tried the following morning at about 6.00 am, it caught fire, and Colin and everyone there fought the blaze with fire extinguishers until the Fire Brigade arrived. The ceiling had to be ripped down to reach the flames, and when all had been doused and the oven investigated, it was discovered that two further pipes towards the bottom of the oven were also faulty. Because it was of old design repairing would have been difficult and costly.

*Sud's 'confectionery' hut, now much enlarged and the home of Colin and Phoebe Price.*

Colin was past retiring age, and the life of a baker is an arduous one. His typical day would begin at 4.30 am, with Phoebe being allowed another hour and a half until she arose at 6.00 am. From then he would work continuously until 1.00 pm. His day could not finish then though, for the shop was still open until 5.00 pm and he still had his booking to do. So the decision was made to close down.

A few months later on a lovely summer evening during a visit to the now empty Bakery I was told by Colin and Phoebe about the day's procedures, and shown the equipment used so regularly over all those years. Some of the tins were still there with Protheroe's stamped on their sides, as were their wrapping papers and tin linings. In their booklet entitled *Protheroe Cakes Stand Supreme*, issued when Miss E.R. Eamonson was owner, were listed Slab Cakes of Special Value. Included were the Wholemeal Cake, which was richly fruited, almond covered and weighing seven and a half pounds; the Dundee Cake; the Ginger Wholemeal which contained cut preserved ginger and was available in nine pound slabs, and the famous Rizza Cake, described as the Queen of Rice Cakes made exclusively with butter and weighing approximately five and a half pounds. Cherry Sultana, Wholemeal Shortbread, Gingerbread, Macaroons and Ginger Nuts. To carry on just makes my mouth water! It states that all were entirely free from preservatives or substitutes and aerated only with eggs, in fact all made as Sud intended with the very best ingredients.

*The Bakery shop a short time before closure.*
*(Photograph by Katrina Thacker)*

I was told the recipe and large quantities used in the bread making. Two seventy pound bags of flour and Dutch vegetable fat combined with the yeast and salt were mixed for twenty minutes before being placed in their four two and one pound tins. After proving and baking for three quarters of an hour, they were placed on trays and put in the bread passage to cool. Then it was off on the delivery van to Stroud, Cheltenham and Gloucester.

Colin always made his own marzipan with ground suet and bitter almonds. He used brown sugar, never white, and butter, nothing less than the best, were the normal ingredients for his cakes. He recalled how his father, William Thomas Price, hauled wood from Leckhampton Station to build property at Whiteway, and how Granny Portlock, Ethel's mother from Bidfield Cottages, scrubbed the shop, bakery and packing room floors for two shillings and sixpence, the whole operation taking her three hours.

Those days are now no more, for after eighty-five years of hard labour it now stands quiet, with the evening sun streaming through its many windows. A place full of memories.

# *Chapter 9*
# THE TITHE DISPUTE

By 1910 there were only eleven houses including Whiteway House on Whiteway, all being on the Wet Ground. The Dry Ground field did have some land allocated to colonists solely for cultivation purposes, but in the main, its use was for the joint purpose of paying off the annual dues to the church called the Tithe.

This was the oldest charge on the land, with one tenth of its produce being taken by the monasteries which were under the Bishop's charge, during very early times so giving them considerable wealth and consequent power. On being attacked by the Danes, then it became necessary to install permanent clergy in the parishes, whose task it became to observe the yields during harvest time, and calculate the amount due from that.

The majority of Whiteway colonists were greatly opposed to this enforced commitment for in their eyes, it was yet another institution depriving the freedom of choice and action which they were endeavouring to obtain, and those at Whiteway were not church users anyway.

So for the colony's first decade, they complied with this annual injustice, by allowing farmer Causey to graze his cows on the Dry Ground field, in return for him paying the Colony's tithe in a lump sum with his own. Several years previously, in 1836, the Tithe Commission had issued the Tithe Commutation Act. This was formed to gradually phase out this unpopular enforcement, and the tithe on produce began then to change instead to that of money. Its assessment was linked to the prices on barley, wheat and oats at that time. The previous seven years' yield was taken into account, with a review undertaken annually also.

Payment of the tithe in crops would have given the colonists more control over its collection, because it would have involved practical growing of the crop, inspection by the clergy, and its subsequent transportation. The Act in fact worked in Causey's favour, because the money transaction was invisible to colonists who wanted to redeem the Tithe land.

The resentment felt by so many, particularly those at Whiteway, did not diminish during those intervening years, so when an idea arose which it was thought might solve the problem for once and for all, it was taken up, sorted out and worked at in a mighty, combined effort, until reaching its proper conclusion.

The proposal was that if the Vicar of Bisley was agreeable, perhaps Whiteway could accumulate enough money to pay off their tithe dues in one large sum to the Church, so enabling them to be permanently free in the future from this commitment. They had begun to realize also that the land which Causey had been using all those years, would be more valuable financially to them if they used it to grow crops on instead for an income. The produce could be sold, and the proceeds used for their new scheme.

Sinclair, on the Colony's behalf, went to see the Vicar of Bisley with the proposition and on his return reported that the amount to be paid had been agreed upon and the scheme could go ahead. Farmer Causey was not happy when he was asked to give up his grazing land, with very good reason for it was soon discovered that for many years the promised tithe money had not been paid at all on the colonist's behalf by him, a fact which dismayed all those who had tried to remedy their dubious reputation of the early years.

Sinclair then personally undertook to collect the Colony's tithe money during the interim, so that all would be as it should be, with no further misunderstandings.

March of 1910 saw the tithe land ploughed and sown with barley. Mugglestone however, held a plot of land nearby which he used for his chickens, and despite being told, made no effort to stop them getting into the growing crop and damaging it. The result was that one Friday morning when it had happened yet again and Sinclair saw two of Mugglestone's hens causing havoc amid the barley, and Mugglestone nowhere in sight to prevent them, he went home and got a gun, and shot the pair of them there and then.

This sort of action would almost certainly have caused a considerable amount of disapproval a few years before, but those who had taken advantage of the settlers with their selfish attitudes, had caused many colonists to change their way of thinking, and so instead of the reprimand Sinclair would have received, now he had thanks.

Happily, despite these set backs, the crop survived and was soon ready to harvest. Ted Adams, Will Sinclair, Peter Howarth and Peter Mylles volunteered to do the mowing, with Bea Adams, Kate Mylles, Leah and Matt Kavanagh, and the road man George Clutterbuck agreeing to follow on behind to bind it into sheaves.

The following January it was decided that they would thresh the barley themselves. This resulted in five and a half quarters at 22s 6d, two quarters at 20s, with the remaining straw fetching £4 4s 0d. Ted Adams bought a small amount of grain for himself, which cost him 4s 0d.

Hoping for a greater yield the following year, the College of Agriculture at Cirencester was consulted in the autumn on the best types of manures and seeds to use, and following their advice the land was fertilized with superphosphates and sown with wheat.

Farmer Hawkins who farmed at Bidfield Farm, drilled in the wheat for them, and some volunteers spread the manure.

Bold George Mackenzie with yet another of his ideas, thought that it might be worthwhile to pay those colonists who had helped out with the clearing of the land for the work they had put in, so that those who had not made the effort to do their bit might be shown up. But even though many with aching limbs and bad backs probably thought the same way, nothing was done and the matter was dropped. Mugglestone's hens were unable to menace the crop this year, as he had left the Colony and returned his land.

Instead the offenders were far greater in number, being the wilder species of feathered friend and unable, like their domesticated relative to be contained within a wire fence. So after Sinclair's success the previous year it seemed necessary to be equipped for any troubles that might lie ahead, even to the lengths of going completely against the ingrained principles that most held. So hoping that Sinclair would be able to repeat his sure aim and cure the impending problem, fifteen shillings was made available for the purchase of a converted Snyder gun. All were certain it would be capable of achieving wonders and save their crop.

That October after the harvesting and threshing, nine quarters of good wheat, two quarters of tail wheat, and three tons of straw were obtained from the 1912 crop. The tithe ground that year was ploughed before Christmas and sown the following spring with sainfoin, mixed with clover and grass.

It proved to be worth the extra effort when two crops of hay were gathered from this sowing during it's first year, with Will Stevens supervising the production of the early crop and Sinclair the later one.

As twice the effort required to be expended because of the double crop, and some felt that the initial enthusiasm might have worn a bit thin by the time the second harvest came round, it was decided that this time all helpers should be paid, each receiving according to his asking. The sainfoin mixture crop lasted for five years, with Sinclair paying £9 for the standing crop in 1915 and Fred Kenworthy the same sum in 1916.

Plans had been made for the crop of that year to be harvested by the Colonists themselves, who were thinking of selling it to the butcher at Bisley at war-prices which would without doubt gain them considerably higher profits. But on being told that cut hay was liable to be taken by the War Office, they decided to sell it again as it stood in the field and Fred Kenworthy bought the crop as he had the year before, and did the work himself.

George Allen, vegetarian and former athlete, with many trophies tucked under his belt, and who now cultivated five acres of land with as much energy as he had needed to break walking records, refused to pay his tithe.

*George Allen with his impressive array of trophies. In 1904 Dr Deighton, a meat eater, walked from Lands End to John O'Groats (909 miles) in 24 days 4 hours. George, in order to prove a vegetarian diet was more healthy, completed the walk in 16 days 21 hours 33 minutes. This victory was his final walk!*

He objected on the principle that he felt his freedom was being curtailed by dictatorial methods from a governing body, whom he did not believe in and would never support. In a letter in 1910 on this particular subject he wrote,

> To the people of Whiteway,
> I think the time has arrived when I ought to tell you exactly how I stand and by doing so save any unnecessary friction . . . I do not regard myself as a private owner of one yard of land and never have done, but I do reckon that no-one either on this place or off has the right to dictate to me in any way as to what I shall do, either in my home or out of it . . . I don't ask for freedom I claim it and give every other person the same freedom . . . As to the tithe, I have never yet supported a parson and never shall, no matter what the result is.

After a meeting held especially to deal with this matter, Jeannie Straughan ended up by paying the money owing herself.

The Tithe money was invested in the Post Office where it accumulated a modest amount of interest. Sinclair felt that if it was transferred to the War Loan instead, a far greater interest could be earned so benefitting the

*George cultivating his land at Woodview. Remarkably, from this poor soil, enriched by George with leaf mould and compost, he produced enough vegetables to sell weekly in Stroud. During the war he refused to increase his prices, and personally gain from the situation.*

common cause. But when he put his suggestion forward, it was received with total disbelief. He reminded them that in his eyes the Post Office and the War Loan were the same thing, as both were used by the Government, but as no one could be convinced by this argument, then the money remained where it was.

In 1917 Fred Kenworthy took the crop as he had done previously, and preparations for the redemption of the land were set into action. Sud and Sinclair had been to see the Vicar of Bisley once again and, in accordance with the Board of Agriculture's rules, notices were put up to inform the general public of their intentions, so giving anyone with opposition to the move a chance to object.

When the time came round the following spring to make an offer for the crop, Sinclair made a more than generous offer of £22, which he hoped would be enough to enable the tithe to be redeemed that very year, so setting Whiteway free from the Church for ever. Whiteway had been obliged to pay five pounds to the Bisley Parish as tithe money on their land every year. Now, in 1918, the accumulated money of eight years' labour had reached the agreed sum of £125.

This was handed over to the Vicar of Bisley on 13 March, a landmark in Whiteway's history. Unfortunately history has shown that this was not the best time for the Colonists to redeem their land as 1918 was the year when the Tithe payment was at its very highest. Also this struggle for freedom proved to be an expensive affair, as the Board of Agriculture also required recompense for their involvement in the transaction, which resulted in another £8 4s 0d being cast in their direction.

Regardless of all else, this combined success proved to those doubters that the communal spirit of Whiteway had not died, but still existed when a necessity to revive it occurred.

Rather unfairly those who lived on Little Meadow continued to pay their dues to the Miserden Parish for another ten years until Jeannie, fed up with it all, finally complained. Their land was redeemed for £18 3s 0d.

There were now several acres of land on the Dry Ground vacant, and it was decided that five of them should be made available for new settlers that year. Interestingly it proved well not to wait, for it was not until 1960 that all land was redeemed, fully forty-two years after Whiteway's accomplishment.

# *Chapter 10*

# THE BUILDINGS AND PEOPLE ON THE DRY GROUND

The Tithe redemption period had included the First World War years. Little in the way of building had been attempted as money and resources were short. The country as a whole being in a state of general upheaval.

The Dry Ground land, hitherto not required for residential use, had acquired its first habitable building in 1910, tucked away from the tithe land, up in the uppermost corner, where state socialist and innovator, George Mackenzie lived, with his wife and two teenage sons.

The custom, on being granted land, in this period of Whiteway's history, was a system where one pound an acre was paid as a deposit on allocation, which was returned on the year's completion minus the rates and tithe. A gallant attempt to raise these enforced commitments.

George, having complied with these necessary requirements, built his home, in later years christened The Rowans. It must be explained that the early houses on Whiteway were rarely given a name, but were referred to by

*Retreat Lane, or the Dry Ground Road, viewed from its entrance. Note Flossie's sign for teas.*

colour, situation or the owner's name. In fact the bungalow then is still The Bungalow today even though it boasts two storeys.

George's home was built from wood, and it became considerably stronger when encased in a layer of bricks later on. He cultivated his land and had many ingenious schemes over a comparatively short period of four years. Although he was not around to see some of his ideas reach fruition, he had planted the seed, which grew with time and money, into something worthwhile, as we will see in later chapters.

It was with regret that he felt compelled to leave the place where he had pushed in his roots, but to him it was a necessary move. In a letter written to the Colony on the 20 August 1914, he explains,

> I was making a fair living and was progressing at a fairly good rate, but during the last twelve months, I had a very unpleasant feeling of insecurity. Take recent happenings: Will Cole's rain barrel, Peter Howarth's cabbages, potatoes from Hodge's ground, and the morning I left I heard that Clutterbuck had lost a lot of potatoes. During March and April it was reported to my wife, that while she was away purchasing milk, a certain individual living on the colony, was seen to be searching the nests of my breeding pens presumably for eggs. I could mention many other cases of colonists complaining of their fruit etc disapearing, but I think I have mentioned enough. These things are generally known but no steps are taken to stop it.

He continued,

> I decided to leave Whiteway much to my regret, because the first two years of my stay there, were about the happiest I had lived, with the freedom from exploitation which I enjoyed there, but since then the exploitation has returned.

So Whiteway lost one of its good colonists because of its views of 'What's mine is yours', and the actions of an unscrupulous fellow, who ignored his conscience and took it at face value.

Fred Large came a year before George's departure, and was his nearest neighbour. He held land in the other far corner, towards the Miserden estate woods, and with reasonable access to water. Billy Burns, a factory worker from South Ealing was its previous holder, but when he had failed to use or occupy it for well over the twelve months probationary period he was sent a letter by the secretary, Peter Mylles, informing him that if it was not used by Christmas 1913, then he would be asked to resign his land.

That September Fred Large was allocated Burns' land, and following a valuation by Sinclair and Peter Howarth of the few crops of any worth growing on the plot, 14s 6d was handed over as compensation to Burns, and Fred installed himself.

Fred was a man of thirty-three, an anarchist who hailed from Walthamstow. He was by trade a house painter, and before moving to Whiteway had previously lived for a while at Bunnage, a couple of miles away towards the Camp. He bought part of the Daneway Estate Office for his living accommodation, and after re-assembling it on his chosen spot, he painted its roof red, which caused it to be known as The Red House or Red Roofs.

Fred Large's family matched his name, numbering six, three of each gender. They were Ida, Harry, Willy, Cecil, Elsie and Mabel.

Fred remained on Whiteway until 1926, during which time his wife left him and moved to Leamington. He decided to emigrate to Canada.

The year following Fred's arrival on Whiteway, in 1914, two former members of a colony at Brussels were passing through Stroud after a holiday in Cornwall. On realising that 'The Whiteway Colony' which they had known of since 1903, but never seen, was nearby, they made a detour to visit it, and being of a kindred spirit with those here, they were welcomed with open arms as old friends. The evening was spent in animated conversation and plans made for Eugène Gaspard Marin and his wife Jeanne, to join Whiteway later in the year.

At a special meeting held the following day they were allotted Hodge's former cultivation land on the entrance to the Dry Ground. After returning to Belgium to sort out their affairs and prepare for the move, they came to live at Whiteway permanently later that summer, in a hut partially built for them by Sinclair and Dennis Boynton. The house took four months to build, from June until its completion on 4 October 1914.

The house consisted of three rooms, with a step ladder leading to the attic above. Four years later, another larger room was added, with a staircase to the attic. This was made by Jeanne's son Gustave, who lived there with Nellie Latimer.

Gassy was in poor health and suffering from TB, but with fresh air, a vegetarian diet and Jeanne's nursing, he recovered amazingly enabling him fourteen years later in 1928, to embark on a World Tour, which although initially was intended to be of three years duration, gradually became extended until it reached a full ten. He travelled by bicycle and on foot, living with the people he met, and involving himself in their cultures. Everything on his trip was recorded in detail and in French. Only his letters home were written in English. In fact Gassy recorded everything he did,

*Jeanne, Gassy and Gustave.*

*Jeanne at La Bosketo, taken in July 1957.*

whether it was written in his small neat hand, or sketched in pen and ink, it was there in detail for future reference. His main subjects were sociology and anthropology, but his interests and researches covered a wide range, from the study of windmills to calculations of time.

The integration of those from different nationalities, socially and academically was important to him, and because of this he began a Communal Holiday Home in 1927 on his land at Whiteway. Africans and Asiatics could combine together in a mutual atmosphere and share their views. This was called Alan Did, meaning Flag Ignorer in Esperanto. Among the guests during the first year were two Samalis, a Zulu, a Japanese, a Chilean, five Frenchmen, a German, a Russian and one English.

Jeanne who was older than Gassy died in 1962, at the age of ninety. Gassy continued living at La Bosketo, the name he had given to their house, which translates as Little Grove in Esperanto. Today it is Lucifer Lodge, the contrast in meaning could never be greater.

Flossie Davies came to Whiteway in 1917 from Sheepscombe. Her father was a footman, and her mother a Court dressmaker. Her uncle was Scott, the wheelwright, and her grandfather owned a lot of property around

*The Retreat viewed from the front garden.*

Sheepscombe. After returning from Africa where she had emigrated on her marriage, and where her four children, Lottice, Ray, Ernest and Wilfred were born, her marriage had broken up. With two of her children, and another joining later, she sought refuge with Bea Adams at The Bungalow.

As she had no money something needed to be done. Gassy and Jeanne relinquished a fifth of their garden in her favour. Rachelle Sinclair supplied a one room hut, which Will Cole erected, dividing it up form two rooms. Assistance was offered from various quarters, and soon Flossie was able to move in with Wilfred, Lottice and Ernest. Ironically Ray the child who most resembled her, remained with his father.

Sud gave her a job at the Bakery, and as she found her feet, she enlarged and improved her house. In 1919 when the Tithe land was opened, and there was more land available, she acquired another acre to add to that already held, and cultivated and nurtured it. She expertly turned the quarry there into a large rockery.

She too took in paying guests, and opened a Tea Shop in 1924, a full tea being available for two shillings and sixpence. When her cooking skills became known, visitors such as cyclists and those with rambling clubs came in abundance, especially during the summer months.

Lottice remained unmarried and lived with her mother. She worked at the Bakehouse for many years, and sadly died of cancer just as she retired. Ernest emigrated to Canada, but came back for a while in 1934, when he

*Flossie Davies.*

was granted a part of the Red House land. He built himself a bungalow there, before selling it to Bill and Dolly Payne, and returning to live abroad. Wilfred, her other son, lived on Whiteway with his wife Vi, at Meadoways, further up the Dry Ground lane, but he too died early in life in 1955. Flossie never left Whiteway, living here until she died in 1969. She named her house The Retreat.

George Barker moved next to Flossie in 1918. He and his wife Minnie came from Bristol. They had no children. Their home was made from two army huts, placed end to end on the edge of the track running straight through the Dry Ground. One was used as living accommodation, while the other was a type of workshop.

George was a little man with a fiery temper, whereas his wife, contrary to her name, was a large woman, the daughter of a fisherman. George could turn his hand to anything, and he loved gadgets. His house was stuffed with bric-a-brac, and he lived in chaos. He even kept his day old chicks in his cellar. He built himself a radio set and owned a gramophone. Those who were lucky enough to be invited there, could enjoy home made cakes and scones while they listened to the entertainments. He also built a generator from which he ran electricity to his chicken houses, which were situated in the quarry at the bottom of his garden.

George Barker once owned a three wheeler Morgan car, which he turned over on Leckhampton Hill. He managed to get it home and into his garage where by the light of a candle he scrutinized the damage. This haphazard method of illumination set his car alight and George, anxious to save his garage, dragged the car out onto the road where it burned away until a blackened twisted mass remained. Perhaps it was this that prompted him to instal electricity.

He never used this form of transport again, preferring instead a motor cycle combination on which he travelled to Dowty's at Arle Court wearing his favourite type of footwear, sandals! While employed at Dowty's he worked on a lathe, and was very much involved with the trade unions, eventually making Shop Steward.

George could be difficult, and he and Flossie could not stand each other. This was made even worse when George shot two of her hens, when they dared to stray onto his ground. Once when Whiteway was involved in a mammoth colony clean up and George had been asked repeatedly to no avail, to remove his now derelict garage from his quarry as it was an eyesore, five authorised colonists left the monthly meeting, then and there, and did the job for him, putting it neatly in a pile at the back. George complained to the police, which resulted in summons being served on those 'guilty', and a court case in Stroud Petty Sessions Court later that month.

Wally Clark, then occupying the Red House, photographed the scene of the crime depicting the remains of George's garage, to show to the Court as evidence. It was not required however, when the Bench in their wisdom decided that the issue was so trivial, it was not worth bothering about. All five were discharged, with only the solicitors and Wally's photograph to pay for.

It has been said how if in the mood, George would strip off to do his gardening, especially when dignified maiden aunts were visiting their relatives eager to show the respectability of the once dubious colony.

Cantankerous though he sometimes was, on other occasions he was an asset to the colony, particularly at the time of the bidding and building of the Hall. With his quick mind he was able to work out a roof structure, which dispensed with most of the upright supports necessary in the original construction, thus creating a considerable open space, invaluable when large gatherings are assembled. What's more he did it from all the existing materials at hand, with no extra cost incurred.

George left Whiteway to live and work in Cheltenham, where later he died, but not without leaving in the true George style. He created a situation of muddles and letter exchanges, eventually resolved when his land was allocated to someone else. Therefore traces of George were removed for ever, but his house, North End remains.

Unfortunately for him, he had been sandwiched between two women, Flossie Davies and Emily Wilkinson. She was granted the neighbouring land in 1920, taking it over from Emily Grout, a journalist with a small daughter, who departed leaving her land unbuilt on. She had lived during her short stay at Whiteway with Bea Adams at The Bungalow.

Emily Wilkinson was an anarchist and inclined to be arty, dressing in smocks. She was a retired Post Office employee, specializing in teaching morse code. On her arrival she was accompanied by Fred Dunn, another of similar views, whose controversial articles had been published in the *Voice of Labour*, and *Freedom*, both anarchist magazines. His stay was short lived, and Emily remained on her own, living in the two roomed hut, built for her by Dennis Boynton.

Emily was known as Sis. This was because her brothers were Arthur and Walter Wilkinson, the puppeteers from Haresfield, who visited Whiteway several times, performing their plays in colonists' houses. Arthur was married with two children and Walter, shy and single, lived with them. They all visited Italy, in order to learn about the construction and operation of puppets, which resulted in them building a theatre at their home in Haresfield on their return, where performances took place with puppets created specifically for the play or opera in which they featured. The greatest care was taken in their modelling and dress, and very impressive they looked on completion, as they were usually all of three foot high.

Walter usually worked the puppets alone which, as he was a shy man, must have proved quite an ordeal for him. The performances were mainly based on legends and fairy tales, although when the need arose, one specially written to fit the occasion would be created. Rhoda Desmond, Gassy and Jeanne's daughter-in-law knew the Wilkinsons from her childhood and puppet shows were held both in her kitchen and at La Bosketo. Tom Keell Wolfe can remember seeing one at Gassy's when he was about six years of age, which would have been in 1922. The puppets then were modelled to represent his father, Gassy and Jeanne.

In the early 1980s the BBC filmed the life of Walter Wilkinson, which was broadcast over several weeks and called *The Peep Show*. Roy Hudd played Walter, and Sheepscombe and Whiteway were both involved in its making. Several children and a few adults had the opportunity to take part, and although excited at the commencement of the day's filming, by the end

*An older George with 'Sis' Wilkinson.*

*George Allen's house at Whiteway, built in 1904 and called Woodview.*

*George's house after removal to Ross-on-Wye, enlarged and remamed Concord.*

*Tom Keell.*

of a hot and sticky afternoon, most children were fed up, and wishing that those children from the twenties had not had to wear such hot clothes. My son particularly was greatly relieved to shed his tweed jacket, bloomers and button boots.

Later when the film was completed and everyone as well as the weather had cooled down, we eagerly assembled in front of the television waiting for the scene that was to bring us fame. It was difficult to distinguish the characters in the darkness of the Hall where the shooting had occurred, but the fleeting glimpse we thought was us was but of shadowy forms. Simply not worth the effort of getting a special hair cut for!

In 1923 after forming a friendship with George Allen, who converted to a similar smock type attire, completely out of character from his earlier more conventional dress, Sis left Whiteway with him and his house, Woodview, which they dismantled ready for re-erection at The Lea, Herefordshire. Unlike George Barker, this George left nothing behind for the colonists to clear.

Emily sold her house, today called Rivendale, to Tom Keell, editor of *Freedom* and Lilian Wolfe.

They were unable to occupy their home for the first few years after their purchase, as they needed to be in London to run the magazine, son Alec Cummings and his family lived there instead. Tom Keell Wolfe, son of Tom and Lilian, was well acquainted with Whiteway, for he had visited many times as a child after his father had heard of Nellie Shaw. Over a period of time he stayed at Rachelle's, Flossie's, Basil and Mary's, and Gassy and Jeanne's.

He can remember being transported up to Whiteway on Gustave's motor bike when he lodged at Gassy's home, going into their garden by an entrance on the corner, not from further down the lane as we do today.

Tom Keell's first contact with *Freedom* was in 1898, and within five years of his involvement with it he had become both compositor and manager. Before long, he was taking control of the business side, and the acting Editor's role, an unenviable task for such a paper during the war years.

Tom Jnr was born in 1916, a few weeks after Lilian was released from Holloway prison, where, after her trial at Clerkenwell Police Court she had been kept in the hospital wing because of the imminent birth of her baby. Tom had been tried there as well, preferring to spend three months at Pentonville instead of paying the fine. Their crime was the one of reprinting and distributing a four-page anti-war article written by Fred Dunn, called *Defying the Act*, Tom did the printing and Lilian dealt with the distribution.

Tom did the majority of the work on *Freedom* until he officially retired in December 1926. The following year the offices they had used at 127

*Lilian Wolfe.*

*Tom Keell Wolfe.*

Ossulston Street had to be vacated, ready for demolition by the Council. So the decision was made to close the paper down. So when Lilian and Tom moved up to their home at Whiteway, *Freedom*'s press and equipment moved up with them.

Tom's time became taken up with cultivating his land, and Colony affairs, taking on the role of Colony Secretary, but as there was still an interest and a demand for the magazine, he went ahead on his own and published fifteen issues of *Freedom Bulletin* over the next five years from Ray's former Carpentry Shop next to the Workshop.

However, the tranquillity of Whiteway was not sufficiently stimulating for someone who had faced controversy for the majority of his life, so when he was asked to edit *Italia Libera – 'Free Italy'*, and *Spain and the World* he took it on. It was while he was involved in this work that he suffered heart failure and died in 1938.

Lilian who had devoted her energies meanwhile to running the Sunshine Health Food Stores in Stroud, continued in Tom's footsteps with the

*Lilian's 90th birthday party in Whiteway Hall. Back: Rene Macdonald, Fred Foster, Pat Elliott, Robert Mitchell, Mrs Mitchell, Gassy, Elsie Pope, Eileen Rosden (Baba), Arnold Miller, Marcel Morand, Fran Miller, Richard Wolfe with girlfriend, Alan Usher (partly hidden behind) Lill Smith and friend, with Rene Mardell on the edge of the picture. Middle: Leonie, Peggie Foster, Nellie Inman, Elfie Clark, Mary Robert, Nellie Morand, Elsie Maxfield, Alan Maxfield. Front: Dedeé Usher, Mary Workman, Joy Evans, Lilian Wolfe, Jose Wolfe, Tom Keell Wolfe.*

production of *Freedom*, working in the health stores during the week, and then travelling up to London at the weekends to do her share on the magazine. Finally in 1943, at the age of sixty-seven, she gave up the Sunshine stores completely, leaving its running to Lilian Smith, and Mary Hill from Cranham, and devoted her amazing energies over the next twenty-five years to the many activities of *Freedom*'s production at its various premises in London. She was a regular attender from 1958 in the Aldermaston marches, often suffering arrest as a result.

On moving to Cheltenham to live with her son Tom who is a Naturopath and his wife Jose, she sold her house to Arnold Miller and his wife Fran. Arnold had been a friend of Francis Sedlak in his youth and so was no stranger to Whiteway's culture. Lilian died on 28 April 1974 at the age of ninety-eight. A marvellous woman, who had persistently upheld the values which she felt were so important.

The final house built on the former tithe land in 1919 was The Croft. It was constructed by Julian Morand, a Frenchman and a conscientious objector.

Constructed is indeed the only word that can be applied to this unique dwelling, for it was made entirely of bacon crates. These were transported from a London market and assembled, just like building bricks, at the end of their land near the road.

Julian, a mechanic by trade, with his wife Dorothy Stafford and baby, Stella, lived in it there for about a year. Then for some reason known best to themselves they dismantled the lot and rebuilt it at the opposite end of the plot, which is where it stands today. Dorothy was the first of the school teachers at Whiteway, but only taught for just over a year, when she left to live in Malaga after the breakup of her marriage to Julian in 1921.

Julian left for London, selling their house to Stormont Murray and Ruth Wood, a school teacher. The seven houses: The Rowans, Red Roofs, La Bosketo, The Retreat, North End, Rivendale and The Croft commenced the further development of the Dry Ground Field.

# *Chapter 11*
# THE SCHOOL

With the availability of the Dry Ground land, and the consequent arrival of another generation of colonists, it seemed sensible that Whiteway should have its own school. During previous years, children had the choice of either walking down to Sheepscombe, which, during the very early years the majority did or along to Miserden where suspicion reigned.

Mr Jolly, headmaster at Sheepscombe and his wife Gertrude had always had good associations with the Whiteway settlers, combining with them in social activities from their days at Bidfield in 1899.

Leonie bravely attended Miserden school. She had learned to read and write at home under the supervision of Dinah Partridge, Will Cole's wife, who was staying with them at Woodcot in around 1912. She was eight years old on admission and on arrival was placed in the class for five-year-olds, but was swiftly upgraded when it was discovered that she was of a higher standard than many older than she, who had been there for a whole lot longer. She stayed until she was fourteen, then left to help at home.

Sud and Jeannie Protheroe sent their girls, Elfie and Dods to Maimie Lediarde's private school at Laburnham Villa Sheepscombe, previously the Old Bakery. The Protheroes and the Lediardes had been friends before Mr Lediarde's death, when they had farmed at Climperwell. Then Mrs Lediarde gave up the farm and moved down to live at Sheepscombe with her daughter, Maimie, who ran her school there. Maimie later married Jeannie's brother Will, so this might explain why Sud chose to pay for the education of his daughters.

Thus in 1920 an idea was put forward for the formation of Whiteway Modern School. It was thought that the school would not be exclusive to those children from Whiteway but open to those from outside also. These could be boarders, living in Colonists' houses, and sharing in outings, holidays, and anything else that was available on the Colony. The only difference between the two sets was that the boarders would be paying and the Whiteway children would not. It was thought that for the present only those over eight years old should be admitted.

There was an abundance of skills, both academic and practical, available from the community in the twenties, for a group of people from the Holt Colony in Norfolk had come to join, after an invitation to set up a Handicrafts Guild with the other crafts people already here.

*Cover of school brochure showing Bea Adams' Bungalow.*

A prospectus was designed and produced, giving all relevant information concerning the new school. On its front cover was a photograph of Bea and Ted Adams' house, with a group of settlers of all ages, conversing together outside, while on the back of the booklet was a photograph of Meadow Cottage, depicting a cottage in peaceful English countryside. Its first page gave an explanation of the atmosphere to which those parents sensible enough to choose this progressive education for their offspring would expect to find.

I quote,

Altitude: 800 feet.
Climate: Very salubrious.
Location: On the Cotswold Hills . . .

Scenery: Undulating meadow land, wooded ravines, sparse farms and hamlets.
Human Surroundings: People who, in an attempt to get away from the unhealthy influences of modern commercialism, have gone back to the land and thus escaped many of the stifling conventions which hinder the development of personality. These people hold their land on the principle of possession use only, and though living in separate bungalows, meet often for lectures, study, music and enjoyment of social life generally.

The new school was designed to encourage initiative and natural abilities through daily living and co-operation with one another. This was combined with the pupils' own researches obtained through books and nature. There was to be no dogmatic teaching regarding religious or political issues, and no punishments or rewards. All students would be judged separately according to their progress, and this would be enhanced with visits to factories, places of interest and through games.

The subjects on offer were many and varied: English and mathematics, physics and chemistry, cosmography and physiography, geography, sociology and history. Also languages, shorthand, handicrafts which included gardening, carpentry, weaving, needlework, and basket making, together with a selection of the arts including drawing, painting and music. If desired, extra tuition would be available in choral singing, orchestra playing, chamber music and theory, and all the classes throughout the syllabus were to be small, never exceeding six students.

Many of the subjects offered were to be taught in the homes of the teachers conducting them, of which there were ten. The boarders were offered accommodation in the bungalows of Colonists, a vegetarian diet taken in the open air if possible, and a holiday with other Whitewayans at a camp at Harlech, North Wales where beautiful scenery, safe bathing, wonderful fauna and flora on the sea shore and mountains could be enjoyed, as could good music in the form of organ recitals.

This holiday was available to Whiteway Colonists for three years, when George Davidson, former co-director of Kodak, welcomed whoever wished to avail themselves of his offer, to spend three weeks during August and September in the grounds of his mansion, Wernfawr. Excursions, picnics, and musical evenings often with famous musicians performing could be enjoyed. All money was combined and chores shared equally. The cost of this unique holiday opportunity was just £1 a week plus railway fares.

The cost for the boarders which included accommodation and tuition was £20 a term for those under twelve and £27 for those over.

*Some Whiteway colonists on holiday at Harlech in 1919.*

The School opened on 20 September 1920 with a fair proportion of Whiteway children, whose tuition was free, and just two paying boarders, Kenneth Craven and Joyce Large who stayed in Nellie Latimer's room at La Bosketo, for the first few months, transferring to Bea Adams' at The Bungalow at Christmas. The following June, Donald Campbell joined. However he was the only boarder remaining when, after the Harlech holiday, both Kenneth and Joyce left.

Dorothy Stafford the main teacher left at Easter after her marriage broke down, and Stormont Murray having bought their house, took her job on. The final disappointment was the departure of Donald the following May, and the term was ended prematurely with a feeling of failure.

Undeterred and determined to use the skills of those available, Stormont and thirteen others of a similar inclination embarked on Whiteway Summer School in July 1922. This ran for a duration of seven weeks and was aimed at the adult student. The object was, 'To stimulate the modern spirit of willingness, to search out realities and found life upon them; and to provide a congenial holiday environment for lovers of nature and all who seek relief from the conventionalities of town life.'

Offered here were lectures on biology and general science combined with practical demonstrations, six on botany and nature study with a further seven on an outline of psycho-analysis, and sociology, these latter delivered by Stormont himself. Exhibitions played their role, with shows of water colours and art photography and recitals by violin, pianoforte and dramatic readings.

Excursions by foot or motor covered visits to Tewsksbury Abbey, decidedly one for the motor, and Cranham Woods, Painswick Beacon, and Seven Springs, to name just a few.

Those who came ate a meatless diet, lived in tents or bungalows, and paid either 50s a week, or 16 guineas for the full term of seven weeks.

All interested were encouraged to 'Apply early, accommodation being limited.' This first year was apparently successful, but was poorly supported when an attempt to repeat it the second year was made, after which it fizzled out and was not tried again.

After the failure of The Whiteway Modern School that year, autumn came around and the school remained closed because of the absence of fee paying students to keep it solvent. Ruth Wood, a former teacher at Letchworth Garden City, took some of the younger children into The Croft as a temporary measure. In November when she revealed that she and Stormont might need to leave because of financial reasons, a meeting was held at Jeannie's to discuss an alternative solution to the school problem, regarding cost and venue.

A committee of five parents comprising Ruth, Mary Robert, Stormont, Stanley Randolph and Winnie Adams was appointed and a Maintenance Fund, collected weekly, the purpose of which was the upkeep of the school, and a General Fund, for the building of a proper school room were started.

As there was some urgency in the need for schooling to begin, a room at The Long Hut, a large converted army hut from Salisbury Plain, was rented from Will and Polly Light. It was lined and painted with much enthusiasm. An earth closet costing 13s 6d was bought, a stove was purchased, and a rota of cleaning drawn up, which left the general daily duties to the children, and the fortnightly scrubbing to the parents.

Ruth, for the present still on Whiteway and receiving £1 a week, remained the main teacher. She provided her Montessori equipment, and worked every morning on academic lessons, while voluntary teachers contributed towards the afternoons lessons, which consisted of mainly handicrafts, dancing and dramatics. There were eleven pupils.

When Ruth neared her confinement with her second son in 1923, Mary Robert filled in as main teacher, and continued as such until 1930 with only a short break for the birth of her daughter Joy in 1924. The Colony now took over the running of the school and special meetings were held to deal with its business.

There was always a fine line between income and expenditure, and a children's craft account was formed especially to cover the cost of materials. The completed items were sold off at a price slightly above the cost of the materials, so ensuring available money for the next purchase.

Performances of several plays were enacted for the Colonists' benefit. There was Myles Malison's *Paddly Pools*, an open air production on Bea Adams' lawn, with a collection raising 25s, used to buy books and drawing boards. Two plays were especially written by Rhoda called *Christmas Eve*, appropriately performed on that day and *Bogies* which was enjoyed by many on New Year's Eve.

In 1925, a landmark occurred at Whiteway. The building of its communal Hall. It came from the Cranham Sanatorium, and although bid for and bought in December 1924, it was not until Christmas Eve the following year, that it was able to be used as a whole building, and even then no form of heating had been installed.

The schoolroom, collected and planned for, had still not materialized and during the school's three year existence had been transferred three times. In January 1925 it moved from its room at The Long Hut, to Eva Zuker's at Trecarne. When her room was no longer available, then Jeannie volunteered Meadow Cottage instead. These temporary arrangements were unsettling, and so when autumn, and the time for lessons, came round again although the Hall was still incomplete, the School moved in.

There was however a feeling of expectancy in the air because the previous July, Stanley had attended another auction at Cranham, and secured a smaller hut for the school at the reasonable cost of £16 10s. This was to be added to the end of the larger building, and with partitioning not needed for the large Hall, an estimate had been made that there would be enough for the completion of the school room without any extra cost.

In November when the unfinished Hall became too cold, the Christmas Holidays came early, and lasted a full eight weeks before more temporary accommodation was found at Mary Robert's at Wayside and Fred Charles' at Swanwick. Fred taught the older ones on Mondays and Fridays with arithmetic and Esperanto, and Mary took the younger ones on Monday, Wednesday and Friday mornings, as well as the older students on Tuesdays and Thursdays. Wednesday was a free day, when prepared work was done at home.

Gwen, a daughter of Bill Clements, attended Whiteway school. Her father, one of the Clements brothers formerly resident at the Rowans, had moved down to farm at Prospect House, Bulls Cross, on his marriage. Although, not livng on the colony anymore he sent three of his children, Gwen, John and Ray to Whiteway School in 1927. They walked there each day via the Salt Box and Hazle House. They would arrive at the Wet Ground's stream where there was a crossing and from where the drinking water was collected. Gwen can remember Mary Robert, Ivy Adams and Stanley Randolph bringing the children for walks and folk dancing. As the

*Lessons on the verandah around 1928.*
*L–R: Ghislaine Griffiths, Joy Robert, Charlie Portlock, Brian Smith, Jacky Protheroe, Leonie Blackwood, Tessa Marin, Janet Ryall, Sue Ryall, Tupps Protheroe.*

Clements children were unable to return home for their lunch because of the distance, they went to Stanley's house instead, taking with them leather cases divided into two sections to accommodate a drink on one side and a sandwich on the other.

During the summer time, Gassy took the older children on a four-day walking tour in the Forest of Dean and the Wye Valley, and there were the usual May Day celebrations and the Sunday picnics.

It must have seemed an age until the Schoolroom opened properly on 14 October 1926. Money had been collected to fit it with cupboards and shelves and a rota was set up to deal with the lighting of the fire and the emptying of the lavatory bucket. There were ten pupils, with the promise of three more joining in the following March.

With the new school premises came new aims. An Education Committee was established whose duties were not only involvement with school matters but also weekly lectures, musical, drama and recreational evenings in general. The library was still struggling on, and when all suggested activities were taken into account, there was not a day that was spare.

Mary continued in her role as principle teacher, now taking mainly the older ones, and another teacher, Ivy Adams, who came up from Stroud and lodged with the Randolphs was employed to teach the juniors. There was a

*Whiteway School with Mary Robert.*
*L–R: Joy Robert, Maurice (Spud) Morand, Ghislaine Griffiths, Dedeé Morand, Rosemary Randolph, Mary Robert, Olive Morand, –?–, Frank Light, David Randolph, –?–.*

*Collecting clay in Miserden woods.*
*L–R: Joy Robert, Maurice Morand, Rosemary Randolph, Gwen Clements, Ghislaine Griffiths, Dedeé Morand, Ivy Adams.*

need for a separate room with two teachers in attendance, so a partition erected at the west end of the Hall, provided each teacher with her own classroom. With this enlarged facility, pupils from outside were being admitted, so making ten full-time and four part-time students on the register in 1930.

French lessons were introduced with Andree Griffiths as teacher, and also folk dancing with Miss Hodenburg from Sheepscombe, both of which proved extremely popular.

In June 1930 Mary resigned. She had worked long and hard through a period of continuous upheaval and challenge and was heartily thanked for her efforts. Ivy became full-time and Andree worked two extra afternoons in addition to her voluntary work.

Then numbers began to drop. This situation was made even worse when parents were informed that if they wished their child to sit for a County Scholarship, allowing them entry into a secondary school, the ruling was that they should attend an elementary school at eight years of age, so the two compulsory years could be spent there. Miserden was the school provided for the purpose in this area.

On Ivy's departure at Christmas in 1931, five children had already been withdrawn, and there were fears that others might leave also. As it was, only five remained to continue after the holiday. Whist drives and dances were held to boost the school's depleting funds – a situation made even worse by the decrease in students.

Andree took Ivy's position on a part-time, six-month trial basis, with a remuneration of 15s a week. When this period was up and considered satisfactory to both her and the Colony, she was offered the post permanently and continued in it, until 1936 when, due to the further drop in numbers and funds the school closed.

The school equipment was carefully stored away, ready for the day when the Whiteway School could be re-opened. Sadly it never was.

# *Chapter 12*

# THE COTSWOLD CO-OPERATIVE HANDICRAFTS

The twenties was a time of new settlers and new ideas, some came to fruition, others came to nought. One that was successful for the eight years of it's duration was The Cotswold Co-operative Handicrafts.

Edward and Beatrice Adams were two of Whiteway's earliest settlers, coming in 1906. Bea originated from Hanley, Staffordshire but moved to Leicester on her marriage to Ted. He was a dispensing chemist, owning a shop in Bradford, but decided to make the move to Whiteway after a visit. They came with their one-year-old daughter Irene, and stayed firstly at Whiteway House and then Woodcot with Walter and Mary, while they were building their home. It was a building with an upper storey, but known as The Bungalow.

They were still at Woodcot when their second daughter Winnifred was born. Ted was frequently away from home, due to his business

*The Bungalow. When newly built it was minus a lean-to extension on its left, and the verandah was open not glassed in, as on this photograph.*

*Bea Adams.*

*Ted Adams.*

commitments, and to supplement their income Bea joined the paying guest brigade. She became successful almost overnight, and soon her home was too small to accommodate all those who wished to stay with her.

A year later another hut was built by Fred Foster in her garden for the overflow. This was known as The Guest House. Later years it earned the names of The Wigwam, and Dear Old Place or DOP.

In 1921, Bea and her daughters visited the Holt Colony near Cromer in Norfolk, in order to learn leather work. While there an arrangement was made with some of its members, to form a Handicraft Guild, and several Holt Colonists agreed to come to live at Whiteway for this very purpose.

Bea purchased a redundant hut from RAF Quedgeley and had it erected by the roadside, a few yards away from her house. This was to serve as the Guild's workshop. When the former Holt Colonists arrived, they were allocated plots of land and proceeded to build dwellings for themselves.

Stanley Randolph, whose craft was sandal making and Rose Rogers with family connections in Sheepscombe were granted an acre of Peter Howarth's land, near Sinclair's cow shed. On this they put two circular corrugated iron huts connected by a covered way, one was used for living and the other for sleeping.

Basil and Mary Robert also came equipped. On yet another of Peter's acres, near the road, they erected the hut which they had brought along with them, used as a weaving shed when at Holt. To this was added a canvas awning which served as their kitchen. Basil was an accounts clerk but now worked at both weaving and leather craft. They were joined by other Whiteway craftsmen, each of whom brought their own particular skills to the Guild.

A meeting was held at Bea's on 15 November to discuss the new venture, with Stanley taking the minutes. The main objective was,

> of working together in a mutually helpful manner, both to consolidate what degrees of efficiency and usefulness could be separately reached by common council and action to extent the same.

The potential members were: Bea, Irene and Winnifred Adams who worked in leather, Mary and Basil Robert also leather workers, Nellie Morand with knitting and her husband Marcel with his wrought iron and embossed metal work, together with Rose Rogers and Stanley Randolph, sandal makers. There was another leather worker, Kathleen Keene, and Ray contributed his craft of woodworking, which he did from his carpentry shop built to the end of the Adams' workshop.

A bank account was opened in the name of the Cotswold Handicrafts and note paper was printed.

*Winnie and Rene.*

*The Workshop with The Bungalow and the Guest House (DOP) behind. Taken from a half-tone copper plated block print, reproduced by Katrina Thacker.*

*The Randolph huts.*

*Stanley Randolph working at home.*

At another meeting a week later the pricing of completed articles was discussed, with the outcome that all members should provide their own materials and equipment, and ensure that all expenses, including time and labour, were taken into consideration in the selling price.

A fund was also established. This was the Common Fund, from which expenses incurred by the guild as a whole could be drawn, including such things as advertising, writing paper, books and exhibitions. To set the ball rolling, everyone loaned ten shillings, but it was expected that when production began properly and the items were sold, this fund would be self supporting, because two and a half percent of their sales would be fed into it. Nothing was to be sold privately, all was to be sold through the guild.

In all it took over a year to get things in order. During that time, consideration was given to extending membership to enthusiastic unskilled applicants, and consequently Stormont was admitted as a trainee leather worker.

The pricing of goods and rates for labour were a problem at the start, as there was no previous experience to draw upon, but finally it was thought best to have a three-month trial to see how things progressed and then fix a rate. This proved a wise move, for when this period was up, it was simplicity itself to divide the sales money by the combined hours worked, and so set the rate for all, everyone being treated equally.

*Basil and Mary's home Wayside, with kitchen awning.*
*L–R: Bert Platten, Mary and Basil.*

*Ray and Basil in Ray's woodworking shop.*

*Winnie Adams.*

*A design for leatherwork by Rene.*

As the months passed it became clear that it might be more beneficial if each craft had a fund apart from that of the Common Fund, especially for its own needs, so that any costs involving their tools and materials would be covered. By completion of the first year of the Cotswold Co-operative Handicrafts Guild, the total sales of the leather workers amounted to £305.

All members had undertaken other essential duties within the Guild in addition to their normal ones, all vital to ensure smooth running. There was ordering, designing and pattern making, cutting and making up, packing and pricing, checking and dispatching, tooling and staining, stock taking, treasurer's and secretary's work, the rates, taxes and upkeep of the workshop to provide for, and exhibitions to arrange. These were held anywhere from Cheltenham to York, from Newcastle upon Tyne to The Draper's Hall in London.

When the exhibition was held in London, those visitors who came to view the crafts showed more interest in these strange Whiteway people they had heard about, than the crafts they exhibited, and reports appeared in the *Daily Chronicle* and other newspapers here and abroad. Headed 'How the Colony Began', the 11 November issue reports on an interview with Ray,

> a sort of picturesque young giant you expect to meet only in childish fiction. He has long hair and a big beard; he wears sandals and homespun, and a blue shirt open at the neck. His appearance in the street of stockbrokers was sufficiently arresting to cause wonder. . . .

*Ray on his motorbike.*

He told me some things about the Cotswold Co-operative Handicrafts Colony – the free life, 'free' marriages, the entire absence of law and authority – that made me yearn for fuller information.

A description follows of a visit made later by the reporter to Whiteway, with general background on its formation,

Through avenues of beech and larch we drove to the roof of Gloucestershire, and then, on either side of a by-road, came suddenly upon bungalows and shacks, wonderfully variegated, and apparently dumped down haphazard over an area of 40 odd acres. It was like stumbling on a No-Mans-Land of civilization.

*Gassy.*

Gassy was chosen to be visited. The reporter states,

> I found another bearded, sandalled man of striking appearance. Books were open on the table, which was covered with a cloth of fine sacking . . . We sat for more than an hour in the room of that centrally heated frugally furnished shack, its walls lined with bookshelves and adorned by handicraft ornaments.

Gassy explained to him how in the Guild and the Workshops, the people work together happily,

> There is no boss. We call the workshops Snip, Snap, Snob, Chip and Co. Snip is the tailor, Snap is the photographer, Snob is the sandal man, and Chip is the carpenter. We send our goods to art shops, and if a visitor wants a suit of clothes, the weavers weave the cloth, and Snip makes it up.

Then he went to see Sudbury Protheroe 'who lives next door to the Bakery over which he exercises a benevolent supervision.' Sud was the one member of the colony he met who was not fantastically dressed. He was sitting by a log fire in dress shoes and smart riding breeches, and looked more like a MFH resting after a hard day with the hounds than a member of this strange colony. He told how few people leave Whiteway. 'We try to be manuals and intellectuals, but we can realise that only in a certain measure.'

This article caused countless people to write to Kathleen Keene, the colony secretary, enquiring about the possibility of coming to live on this small piece of land where a few lucky people were living a simple uncomplicated idyllic life. Most stressed their love of their fellow man, their conversion to vegetarianism and briefly, towards the end, their lack of money and inability to work too hard due to poor health.

In June 1924, Stormont and Kathleen withdrew from the Guild, Kathleen preferring instead to devote her time to her Tea Shop business. Soon, Winnie and Bea took up hand weaving instead of their customary leather work, with Rene joining them a short while after.

Four years after its conception, in March 1926, Basil and Rene were the only ones working full-time, with Winnie, Mary and Fred Large's daughter Mabel working as part-timers. Ibrahim Ismail from Somaliland or Salah, joined the Art leather workers where he learned book binding under Basil's capable wing, and Bert Mardell joined the Art leather group as wholesale salesman.

By 1927 it was felt that a change should be made partly due to Bea

*Bea Adams, weaving.*

*Basil instructing Rosemary Randolph and Dedeé Morand.*

needing more space in the Workshop for her own family's weaving, so Basil built himself a workshop on his land by the road for his leather work. Everyone who had used Bea's workshop over the years combined together to replace the roofing, creosote the exterior walls and paint the windows, so leaving it clean and tidy for the weavers to carry on their work.

So ended the Co-operative Handicrafts Guild on 7 July 1930. In 1956, Basil and Mary allowed their former workshop to be converted into a home by Joy, their daughter and her husband, Peter Evans. It became known as The Makins. 'Because it has the makin's of a fine home.'

Peter is a carpenter making fine furniture and Joy a carver. Alan their son is an artist metalsmith, and has a forge next to his father's carpentry shop. Marvellous examples of his work can be viewed countrywide, with one of the earliest being in our capital, when he designed and made the gates for St Paul's Cathedral Treasury. He was awarded this commission after winning the Crafts Council Competition. His early years were influenced by Ernest Gimson and Sidney Barnsley, who were members of the Sapperton Arts and Crafts Movement, close by. Alan's inspiration comes from his emotional reaction to the area in which the job he is commissioned to do is situated. As with the early craft movement, his successes have been demonstrated in exhibitions and magazine articles. He also has the advantage of television and wide media coverage unavailable to his predecessors.

*Basil's workshop, now The Makins.*

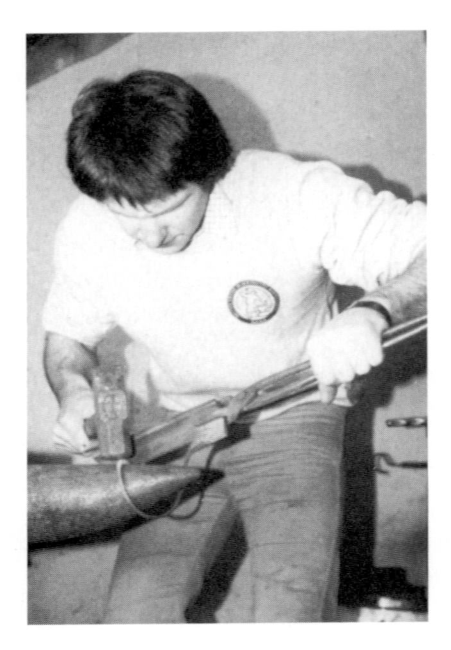

*Alan Evans at work in Whiteway in 1987, forging one of six trophies for the Royal Society of Arts.*

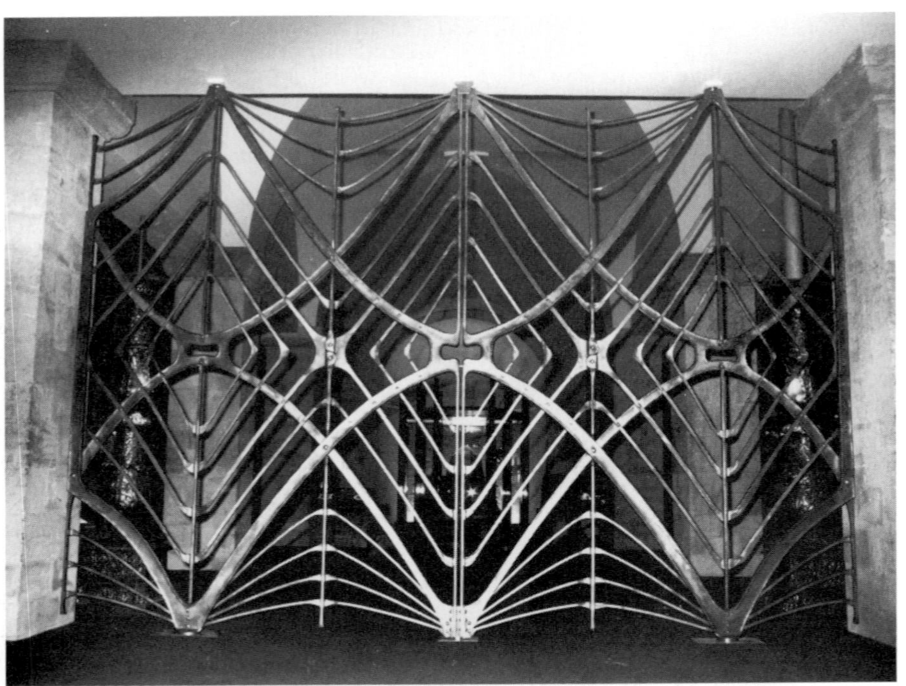

*The Gates for the Treasury at St Pauls in London, designed and made by Alan Evans. Photograph by Alan Evans.*

Other craftsmen at the time of the Cotswold Handicraft Movement preferred to work alone. One was Rhoda Marin, who ran a printing business called The Dodo Press. It was so called after her sister, Dora, who went to New Zealand, remaining there until she died, unlike Fred Foster who, after returning from that self-same country in 1927 was granted a piece of land down by the stream on which he built his hipped roof house on stilts. The upper portion being his wood-working shop with his woods occupying the space underneath where they could season in an airy atmosphere. Here, in sympathy with the traditions of the Arts and Crafts Movement at Sapperton, he created his furniture.

During the early twenties, two other communally based schemes were also embarked upon. The first was the Communal Housekeeping effort in 1921. Four people from Kidlington near Oxford decided to settle at Whiteway, and build a house where the old ways of living and sharing expenses and labour, could be attempted once again.

The Long Hut, in which it was thought that each person should have a bedroom and private living room, while the kitchen dining room, library and further reception room should be used commonly by them all was erected after being brought by lorry from Salisbury. There was even to be a science room. As in Whiteway House, all the house and land work was to be shared, with the land having no boundaries and all, including some held by their surrounding neighbours was cultivated in common.

After barely a year, the scheme broke up with two of the innovators leaving the Colony, and the other couple, the Charles, who were now married moving across to The Croft into rooms offered them by Ruth Wood. The Long Hut was closed down until it was bought by Will and Polly Light who came with their two sons, Dennis and Frank, in May 1922. There was ample room for the Charles now, and they lived with the Lights until they could move into their own house which they were building nearby.

The land was divided according to each dwelling, but the common cultivation continued for a little longer, in the hope that it might encourage other Colonists to involve themselves also in a similar vein. It seems unlikely that the aforementioned did have any effect on this next communal effort, but it might have done, in a minor way.

This was attempted in 1925 and was called the Co-operative Gardening Group. It was devised in order to grow all types of vegetables, and nine people took part. They used 4,711 square yards, and the total hours worked amounted to 1,223. Each worker kept a record of his own hours, and the proceeds were divided accordingly. This effort lasted longer and was more successful than that of the Communal Home, for it was still in existence, although perhaps reduced in members and acreage after 1927.

Gassy's Communal Holiday Home, Alan Did began that year, with a round tin hut arriving on the 5 May to act as additional accommodation for the Asiatic and African venture, which welcomed all to join together to share their cultures and ideas. This proved popular until about 1929. These are a few of the attempts to revive some communal spirit, which some felt had been lost during the twenty years since individuality began.

# *Chapter 13*
# THE COLONY HALL

The most outstanding accomplishment of the twenties was, without doubt, the building of the Colony Hall. Everyone combined in the old spirit of the early pioneers, just as they had done seven years before to redeem the tithe.

It had been plain for some years that a room of some kind was needed where social activities could take place. Many rooms in many houses had been used over the last twenty-five years. We have seen how on George Mackenzie's suggestion, the wash-house had served some use as a communal room, where the club members were able to meet away from their homes, and Bea Adams frequently gave the use of her workshop, which expanse of space was unavailable elsewhere. There had been a false alarm in 1918 when there was talk of a community room on the Old Children's Playground behind Whiteway House, but hopes were dashed when the money promised failed to materialize.

After the auction at Cranham Sanatorium on 30 November 1924 and the consequent purchase of their hut, all colonists young and old turned out on

*Bidding for the hall building at Cranham.*

the following Sunday, armed with an assortment of implements which they thought were suitable for pulling a building apart. Within three weeks the whole building had been dismantled, and transported back to Whiteway on a lorry from Cheltenham, the final load arriving late at night on the Sunday before Christmas.

After discussing the pros and cons of whether the original idea of The Playground, or alternatively Basil's ground near the road was a suitable site for this communal amenity, both were ultimately abandoned in favour of a spot at the bottom of Flossie's land, and there it was that throughout the winter volunteers laid the foundations.

The first section was heaved into position on 10 May and by the beginning of August half the floor was down, the school room partly built and a group of jubilant Colonists gathered together for the first time in their own Hall. In the future, it would be host to every kind of event, social and otherwise, for the next seventy years and more. The weekly collection set up to fund the Hall building continued, and by Boxing Day, the entire hall was opened and a social held.

*Building the Colony Hall.*
*Some of those helping are Jeannie, Salah, Elfie and Fred Charles, with Dods and Rhoda seated in front.*

*Colony Hall with Schoolroom to the right, completed.*
*Today it has no skylights.*

There was still much to be done before it could be considered as complete however, and volunteers came and went depending on their time, circumstances and frame of mind. In all the main building took eighteen months to complete, and in order to actually get it finished, as after initial euphoria enthusiasm can wane, a Hall Committee was formed to deal with all matters relating to it.

The heating, lighting, cleaning, furnishing, decorating and arrangement of functions were all discussed, and brought before the Colony Meeting for their approval. A list was drawn up of the many jobs to be done in order to complete both the Hall and Schoolroom, and tenders obtained for any skilled work. This usually resulted in those chosen only accepting half the money offered, the remainder of the time being donated free.

The list seemed endless and included the erection of a notice board, seating, Hall insurance, the fastening on the door, glass to be put in windows and over hall and school room doors, barrels to be obtained. It continued with a soakaway and three earth closets to be made and a urinal from any left over timber, and the construction of an eight-foot-wide road from the parish road to the Hall. There was also coke to buy for the stove, obtained at two pounds a ton, a shed to store it in, the verandah to glaze and cement and the painting of both the interior and exterior of the building. The outside was duly painted a rich biscuit colour, with the windows and doors ultramarine and the roof red oxide, just as it is today.

*A view of the Hall with surrounding buildings, taken from the top of the garden at The Makins.*

Soon, for the sum of thirty pounds, a secondhand grand piano stood proudly in place. The major portion, twenty pounds, being contributed by a generous friend of the Colony from another village.

All evenings and weekends were booked solid and a caretaker appointed, who was paid £1 a month for his services. There was a drama group, a sports group, folk dancing, Esperanto classes and lectures. The lectures were a regular occurrence, having been organised on a weekly basis since 1920, and were delivered by an invited guest, a visitor just here for a short while or a colonist. In fact anyone who felt confident enough to stand up and talk.

Before the Hall was available these events were held at The Bungalow and Bea's Workshop and continued practically uninterrupted for eight years. The subjects ranged widely from 'Experiences in Poland', to the 'History of Russian Literature', a mesmerizing talk on 'Hypnotism' one week and the revelations of 'The Unconscious Mind' the next. In the series on botany with George Jolly, headmaster at Sheepscombe School, the audience heard about 'The Female Organ of the Plant' in lecture six followed by 'The Male Organ' in lecture seven and the study of both specimens in the eighth.

From 'Life and its Activities' we then had the 'Liquidation of Civilization'. Nellie Shaw and Bea Adams both explained 'Why I Came to Whiteway', a visitor revealed 'How an Outsider sees Whiteway' and Stanley Randolph explained 'Possibilities of Improving Whiteway'. The lectures ceased in 1928 after 341 had been given on nearly as many subjects, with the hope that they might be resumed one day.

*Everyone in costume for a Whiteway drama production, possibly* The Feast of Death *performed in 1924 in Bea's workshop*

*Three of Whiteway's folk-dancing boys. L–R: Harold Palmer, Frank Light and Tommy Maxfield.*

It was now possible to provide tea for the large groups of people who wished to visit Whiteway to see what it and those on it were like. As numbers increased a Catering Committee was created to cope with them, with a Catering Fund opened to manage the profits.

Getting things off to a flying start the first summer were two organisations from Bristol. The Bristol ILP with sixty-two members came in mid June contributing a shilling each towards the Fund and The Folkhouse Players arrived towards the autumn, free of charge.

In 1930 when the reputation of the Catering Committee had grown, six parties came, with the result that tea was served to a total of 199 adults and 24 children. Two years later, in July 1932, a massive party of 250 women and children from the Labour party were catered for by a small team of four Colonists. With an increase in 1934 to eight helpers, the 11 September tea had a mere eighty from the Bedminster Woman's Co-operative Guild. It seems that this tea effort continued successfully for many years, at least until the onset of war.

Every holiday was packed with social activities each group organising events to which all were welcome. Over an Easter Holiday of four days, a typical example of Whiteway entertainment was the Gramophone Group on Good Friday, The School Group taking care of the Saturday and a general Colony Night with communal refreshments on the Easter Sunday. The Bank Holiday Monday event was organised by the Sport's Group, Christmas Day's function included parlour games, while Boxing Day involved the Children's Party in the afternoon, and a whist drive for the adults with games and dancing in the evening. A further dance on New Year's Eve welcomed the coming year.

On May Day, there was the charming Festival with the May Queen's coronation in the afternoon and a folk dance in the evening. Elsie Maxfield from Lancashire brought this custom with her when she came to Whiteway in 1921. All the traditional songs, dances and customs which she remembered from her childhood were taught to the Whiteway children, and faithfully followed each year.

In order to qualify as May Queen, the little girl had to be a Whiteway child, and around ten years old. Some were a year or two older when they eventually sat on the throne, for no one wanted to be left out.

The dress always worn was a Grecian style white silk dress with a long pale green silk train. A crown made of flowers, woven onto a base with a peak at the front passed from one to another each year. Posies were also made with a pretty paper doily underneath to finish the whole outfit off.

A stage was erected at the Schoolroom end of the Hall, and the previous year's queen performed her final duty of placing the freshly adorned crown

*Maureen Light as May Queen with her attendants. Back: Tim Blatchford, Mike Usher, Edward Scott, Philip Toogood, Mike Portlock, Frankie Payne. Middle: Paul Frampton, Barbara Phelps, Maureen (May Queen), Freda Scott, Trevor Carter, Derrick Allen, Judith Mardell, Ann Wolfe, Richard Wolfe, Steve Merrett. Bottom: Mark Frampton, Alice Scott, Rosalind Evans, Sally Evans. Valerie Palmer, Pete Palmer and Jessica Blatchford are the three immediately to the front.*

*A special moment for Frankie Payne, who recieves her crown from Judith Mardell.*

upon the newly appointed queen's head. The Long Hut's lawn was used for the ceremony for its first three years, but when the Hall became available, with all its space, then preparations became more elaborate, with greenery and floral decorations everywhere.

Bluebells grew in profusion in the woods down Wishanger Hill, still do in fact, and these were picked, together with cowslips that were found in the field towards its top. There was the Japanese Cherry tree, one of which could be found in the Adams' garden, its blossom at this time was a must to the decoration, as were Beech leaves, which were young and fresh and green.

The little girl whose turn it was to be crowned, was decked out in her robes at Elsie's house and one can imagine how nervous she must have felt on that short walk down the path to the Hall, where a crowd of colonists and relatives was waiting to greet her!

It was a popular occasion and many, young and old, came to witness this magical day. For a few years there was a short explanation of the meaning of Labour Day, but later this was discontinued.

The first May Queen was Mabel Large and the last one, thirty-six years later, pretty Maureen Lally. As this tradition has now ceased, it is possible to see the May Queen's robe in the Gloucester Folk Museum.

*Maureen Lally, the last May Queen in 1959.*
*Back: Mark Frampton, Frankie Payne, Judith Mardell, Steve Merrett, Enid Maxfield. Middle: May Queen, Rosalind Evans, –?–.*
*Front: Alan Evans, John Burton, –?– Burton, Barbara Phelps.*

*Folk dancers with Elsie Maxfield.*
*Back: Madeleine Mardell, Valerie Tidy, Muriel Portlock.*
*Front: Shirley Carter, Elsie and daughter Enid.*

Rose Rogers was invaluable in her contribution to the May Day celebrations, because she was able to teach the Folk Dancing which she had learned at Letchworth eight or so years before. In fact so popular did this form of dancing become, that a Whiteway Folk Dancing Group was formed, with over twenty colonists of all ages involved. Bea Adams' Workshop was taken over each week for practising, until the time came when the group could move to the Hall. The Folk Dance Group joined the countrywide English Folk Dance and Song Society. This enabled them to send a team to the summer festivals which were arranged by the Gloucestershire Branch, held annually at such places as Cirencester Park, Stanway and Berkeley. Also each year, Rose and Stanley, with Elsie and Lill Smith would travel to London to attend the Folk Dance Festival at the Albert Hall.

Drama had always been a large part of Whiteway's social life from the very early years. Plays were performed in rick yards, in cow sheds, on lawns and in sitting rooms. One fondly remembered was *Chu Chin Chow*, written in 1918 especially for Whiteway by Pan, or Edward Smith, a great friend of the Colony. In fact it was so successful that the following year he wrote another one called *The Whiteway Girl*, a semi musical, which involved a large proportion of the Colonists, who acted out their roles in many comical and inventive ways in the cast. It was performed in the Bakehouse on New Year's

*Poster showing cast.*

Day and was the story of an American who tried without success to buy Whiteway and turn it into a profit-making enterprise.. For many years after it became customary for a play to be performed somewhere on Whiteway, and these included *Gentlemen of the Road*, Bernard Shaw's *You Never Can Tell* and *Candida, The Collaborators, Come Michealmas*, and John Macefield's *The Tragedy of Nan.*

On the availability of the new Hall, a Whiteway Drama Group was formed and the decision to join the British Drama League made. A removable stage was built and scenery, costumes and all the props associated with the acting profession were acquired.

When the membership dropped and performances had to cease, these were stored until its revival, in the 1940s, by Bill Gibson, a trained musical arranger who held drama classes and produced plays for which he wrote both music and lyrics.

The Hall was not only used for leisure activities, it also had its more serious uses, which are expanded upon later.

They can never learn the trick,
Horticulture with a pick,
That makes us fit and strong at Whiteway.
They can never lie in bed,
With the drips that cool the head,
They can never know the bliss,
Using pails for that and this,
For these are the privilige of Whiteway.

*Part of a poem by Bill Gibson, memorized by Dolly Payne.*

# *Chapter 14*
# WHITEWAY'S CONSCIENTIOUS OBJECTORS

One continuing element of the old pioneering spirit had been an objection to compulsory conscription in times of war. It was seen as an infringement of personal liberty. Whiteway had always been sympathetic to such views, and protected and sheltered those of such mind, when the occasion arose.

George Allen came to live on Whiteway in 1904. He built himself his house, Woodview, on Fishpond piece, and on its completion his wife Annie, with daughter Annie, sons Jimmy, Paul and baby Billy all came to live in it. His sons were encouraged to help in the cultivation of his three acres, increased to five around 1910. After his wife died he formed a friendship with Leonie's mother, Alice Birkenhead.

He was a man of strong convictions, preferring to spend a fortnight in Gloucester prison than comply with the National Registration Bill when it was introduced in 1915.

Jim, his oldest son, together with Peter Howarth's two sons, Fred and

*Woodview in about 1905.*

*Dennis Boynton holding the donkey who was used during the building of the road leading to George Allens' house, known by all as 'the donkey path'. Astride him are Leonie's cousin, Billy Allen, Paul Allen, Leonie and Jimmy. The year is 1911 and the distinctive shape of Bea Adams' bungalow is in the background.*

*Jim Allen.*

Jack, tempted with the promise of thirty shillings a week and the love of horses, obtained work in Avonmouth during the First World War years, where horses and mules were being trained for the army. Unknowingly, by this very slight involvement with the Military, they had automatically invalidated any rights of claiming exemption on conscientious grounds.

Fred and Jack unwillingly went to fight, which resulted in Fred dying from dysentery and Jack losing a leg. Jim however, now eighteen years of age and so eligible for enrolment, refused, and consequently spent 112 days hard labour in Wormwood Scrubs. His views were still unaltered on his release, and so he was sentenced to a further six months imprisonment in Gloucester prison.

The story goes that on the day of his release, he was met at the prison gates by his father George, Will Stevens and a bicycle, and leaping onto this he sped back to Whiteway. After hiding for the night in Will Cole's shed, he travelled to Brislington, and then to Ireland. There, armed with forged papers, he worked as a coal trimmer on several ships, eventually ending up in New York. After a stay of one year in Pensylvania, and five more years at the Ferrer Colony at Stelton New Jersey, he spent his final eleven years at the Mohegan Colony in New York, from where he finally decided to return to England.

On his return to Whiteway in 1933, he bought Peter Howarth's old house, The Shack, from the same Will Stevens who had met him with the bicycle all those years before, and lived there until he died, over thirty years

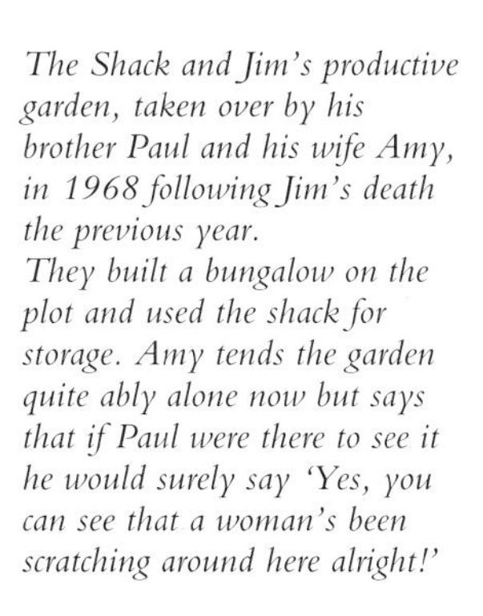

*The Shack and Jim's productive garden, taken over by his brother Paul and his wife Amy, in 1968 following Jim's death the previous year. They built a bungalow on the plot and used the shack for storage. Amy tends the garden quite ably alone now but says that if Paul were there to see it he would surely say 'Yes, you can see that a woman's been scratching around here alright!'*

*Tales of the past in America? Can this be Dennis Boynton sharing memories with Jim?.*

*Dennis Boynton (?) and Jim in front of The Shack.*
*The Shack dates back to 1906. Alec Protheroe departed from Whiteway then, leaving the remnants of an uncompleted house. As stated, some of this was taken down to Sud's ground where it was used for his Bakery building. Peter Howarth from Blackburn, Lancashire, having left his wife, came to live in The Shack, which in all probability was Alec's unfinished house, at this time with his two young sons Jack and Fred. He held a considerable amount of land, both on the Wet and Dry ground. It stretched from Sinclair's farm to the end of Dairy Lane, with more over the road at Wayside and The Makins. He lived there until his death in 1932 when Will Stevens, previously from The Cloisters, purchased it for £15. It was from Will that Jim bought it in 1933.*

later. He never married but devoted his life to cultivating his ground with a variety of vegetables which he sold, and flowers which were always planted neatly in rows. The specialized snowdrops and daffodils which today cover a large proportion of his land were also an absorbing interest.

He said that to return to England after all those years away, was the biggest decision he had ever had to make. To relate the adventures of his many years in America was a pleasure for him and his listener, and the American twang which accompanied his stories lent a liveliness to their telling. Whether seated either side of his stove, sustained with a cup of tea or during the purchase of a bag of potatoes, snippets of his life would emerge. His home is one of the few remaining houses on Whiteway today which is exactly as it was when Jim lived there. The stove along with many other fitments still remain, and even though it is all of twenty-five years since any form of heat has warmed that small hut, the walls of which have absorbed Jim's experiences, the cellar beneath is as dry as a bone.

Will Cole lived on Whiteway but not on Colony land. He was a true colonist in beliefs if not in land holding. He had been a chemist but had turned his hand very successfully instead to market gardening. In appearance he was tall and handsome, and like the others of similar mind and age on the Colony in 1916, he could not agree to the destruction of human life.

In October 1917 he was arrested at his home and charged with being an absentee after he had returned all his calling up notices to the recruiting authorities with 'returned with thanks' written on them. When he had made it plain that he would never join the army, and would furthermore escape if the chance arose, his transfer to Horfield Barracks in Bristol was postponed for four days, until more men became available to accompany him. After arriving at Horfield, he was given a meal, paraded and told that he was free until tea-time. Perhaps they should not have used this particular word, for Will took their instructions at face value and calmly walked out, taking the train to Brislington, and Cardiff, where a friend gave him three pounds and fixed him up with a journey to Dublin.

Once in Ireland, he answered an advertisement for a gardener, and spent the next two years occupied in something that he liked and was able to do well.

Several other men appeared before the Stroud Tribunal. Harry and Bill Clements, also market gardeners on what was George Mackenzie's land, were exempted for six month periods at a time. This was renewed and renewed for as long as they remained in their occupation, and Fred and George Kenworthy fared likewise as farmers and carriers.

Gassy, as a Belgian with indifferent health, had no fears, but when it became known that he was involved with anti-war activities, then his house,

*Will Cole.*

and that of George Allen was raided, and the associated literature seized. He was served with a deportation order, and taken by car to a Belgian prison in London, where he went on hunger strike.

After transfer to a Belgian military hospital in Highgate, where he stayed for eight weeks, it was found that for a variety of different reasons the deportation could not go ahead. The only alternative, therefore, was to return him to Whiteway where his friends were waiting to greet him on an October day in 1917. Henceforth the police took care to watch his movements.

Julian Morand and Ray, another conscientious objector, both came from France, and in order to hide their French identity assumed Spanish names.

Their Spanish papers had been sent to them inside the boards of a box of onions by Barcelona anarchists. On 12 September 1919 they were arrested for this action and their possession of Spanish papers. Following their case, which was heard in Cheltenham law-court, they were sentenced to two months imprisonment in Gloucester prison. France did not recognise conscientious objection, and by refusing to fight they were liable to be shot.

On their release in November a celebration was held by George Barker at North End for them, and for all those objectors who had suffered for their convictions.

In 1942, after Russia had joined in the conflict, a small group of Colonists who sympathised with the Communist party formed themselves into a group, and held fortnightly meetings in the Hall. Those who veered more towards Pacifism also had their group called The Peace Pledge Union, with its first meeting being held at Lilian Wolfe's on 26 July, and at Jeannie's from then on.

That year also Peace Celebrations were held all over the British Isles and Miserden was no exception. Theirs were held on 5 August and Whiteway was invited to partake in the day's festivities. Whiteway felt unable to attend, for as the reply letter states,

> While fully appreciating the kindly spirit in which it was sent, we consider that to take part would be a farce, in view of the general attitude of the British Military Party, and their conduct towards the people of Russia. When real peace dawns, we shall be pleased to join with you in rejoicing.

When the Second World War raised its ugly head, Whiteway was still here as a refuge to those who needed it. The result being that during the early forties it gained new members, some of whom stayed and integrated into the Colony with their families.

The imprisonment suffered by objectors then meant a bed of eight-inch-wide planks set on a framework five inches off the floor topped with an oakum-filled, sacking-covered mattress, porridge and tea for breakfast, and work sewing mailbags. For those with a trade the workshop became the daily workplace, where all tools covered their white painted shape on a board fixed to the wall, so that any missing might be seen at a glance by the warden and sought out. The work varied with anything from general repairs to constructing huts in the prison grounds for use as extra accomodation.

Those in prison as objectors can also remember that hard labour could sometimes mean four cigarettes issued with three matches. Many ingenious methods were invented to deal with that particular problem, from splitting a match into four whilst retaining a minute portion of phosphorus on each strip, a skill rarely needed in the outside world, to igniting a scrap of hankerchief in an old tobacco tin if you were lucky enough to have one, for use later.

Peter Evans remembers buying a return ticket for himself with a single for his conciencious objector friend when he accompanied him on the bus to face the authorities in Gloucester, so sure was he that he would be coming home alone. This action was repaid however a little while later, when the situation was reversed, for his friend was now able to do the same to him when he saw him off on his spell of military service!

As part of the War effort, the sports field underwent a change from its previous usage. The two acres of land on the Dry Ground which had been set aside as a sports field in 1936 as 'a private open space in perpetuity' had been levelled free of tumps and molehills, with any small trees being removed, and much effort and money raised to construct a hard gravel tennis court and cricket pitch.

This was now temporarily abandoned and food and fodder such as oats, wheat and potatoes took over instead. After the wheat had been harvested in the August, Mr Dickinson, the local farmer had ploughed in the stubble, and drawn dribbles in preparation for the potato crop the following year, all for just £2 inclusive. It was then handed over to the colony, whose responsibility it was to obtain the manure, seed potatoes and deal out the profitable results to the Colonists.

A promised thirty-one colonists, armed with buckets and hoes, set to work over a weekend in May and several following evenings, and planted the potatoes until all was done except the headland. The Sunday afternoons chosen for the final planting, dock pulling and fertilizer spreading brought a poor turnout. However, those who did come completed the task as arranged, and a machine to lift the earlies was booked for a Saturday at 2.00 pm.

When October came round, and with it the turn of the main crops for lifting, the weather was so wet that the machine was unable to achieve its purpose, and all had to be dug out and picked by hand. It took until the beginning of December for the complete crop to be harvested, with the result being a smaller quantity than hoped for.

Then after all of the crop was safely stored in the Hall, those helpers who had contributed more labour towards the final result were priviliged by being the first in line on allocation, with the others receiving their share suitably divided afterwards.

The following year when the War Agricultural Executive Committee decided that Whiteway should plant a potato crop again, an arrangement was made with them in advance to send machinery which would plough, harrow, bout, earth and hopefully this time lift the crop, with volunteer colonists providing labour for the setting and picking. On the Sunday before Easter the entire task of setting and manuring was achieved in three and a half hours, due to a most commendable turn out. This was not to last long however, for before the final picking that September, paid help was required. That year a dealer bought the majority of the harvested crop, with those colonists requiring some for their own needs buying at wholesale prices when they purchased a hundredweight or more.

The War also contributed towards Whiteway's first public telephone, put in mainly for the use of Wardens and the Fire Service. It was installed in 1941 in Basil and Mary Robert's Workshop beside the road. When, four years later it was no longer needed for its original purpose, a public kiosk was erected just outside, a distance away of just a few feet, but one which cost Whiteway £4 over five years for the privilege. The telephone exchange to which it was linked was at the rear of Miserden Shop, which was run by Mrs Brown, who was always there to help and give advice when needed. In those days real human contact was available, unlike today with disembodied recorded messages.

Twelve people volunteered to become wardens and night watchmen during the war, three on the non-Whiteway land and nine on the Colony. Others did fire service duty. People were also encouraged to attend a course of six lectures on first aid. The introductory one was held on 24 July 1942, only a night before the first air raid came.

# *Chapter 15*

# WHITEWAY'S SPANISH 'FRIENDS'

During the Spanish Civil War, Whiteway accommodated several men from Spain in their Colony Hall. Britain did not officially offer sanctuary officially to those wishing to escape from this terrible conflict between the rebel Nationalist and Republican parties, for it had investments in Spain and so thought it best not to be involved, and ultimately upset the winners.

In fact as Britain wished to ride with both fox and hounds, it was decided to confine the war to Spain and so avoid any confrontation with Germany and Italy. Its policy therefore was to give no help at all. However, there were some British men who went of their own free will to support whichever party they thought fit, and from about 2,000 who did go, around a quarter died in conflict.

In May 1937, the Basque set up a Children's Committee which resulted in 4,000 children coming to England as refugees. On their arrival at Southampton, homes were found for them from sympathising sources. Also, it was agreed that if anyone would offer accommodation and food to any Spanish men who wished to come, then sanctuary for them would also be found in Britain.

General Franco opposed the ruling Republican Party for three years from 1936, and in March 1939, made his *coup d'etat*, which put an end to the second Spanish Republic. The last resistors left Madrid that same month, and after flying to Manesis, they went on to Gandia where they were transferred onto the warship, *Galatea*. After transfer to the hospital ship, *Maine*, they travelled to London and to Frith Street where those anarchists who were organising things met and welcomed them.

None could speak English, and all were in a pitiful state. Harry Clements, a former colonist, contacted Whiteway about their sorry plight and homes were offered to as many as accommodation could be found for on the Colony. He and Marcel Morand set off for London to collect the men. Harry returned with three and Marcel with another five. Another two travelled by train.

On arrival at Whiteway two slept in Whiteway House, two in Jeannie's Studio and the rest were accommodated in the Hall, with the Schoolroom serving as their sleeping quarters and the main hall for everyday living. On arrival all had a bath and were given clothes, some of which were acquired from firms where colonists worked.

*Our Spanish Friends.*

Nellie Morand set to and mended those items which needed it, and everyone who was able provided food of some sort or another. Joy Evans can remember her mother cooking a pig's head at one time to make brawn with. There was an urgent need for bedding and many blankets were loaned. However when these needed to be returned, word was sent to Miserden to see if they had any to spare, and they obliged accordingly.

Two committees were formed, one of Whitewayans, with Nellie taking on the post of secretary and the other of the Spanish men. Rules were laid down designed to ensure that the minimum of disagreements occurred. Any money which was collected from the Colony was combined with that which came down from London, and Nellie took control of it, giving it to whichever Spaniard was due to do the cooking that week.

It was decided to mention even the smallest misunderstanding, and so that all matters concerning their well being, money and work could be talked over, a monthly meeting was arranged between both the colonists and the Spaniards. Personal affairs were never included in these discussions, as it was thought that the Spaniards' privacy should be respected. It was hoped that if consideration was shown to them then it would, in turn, be returned to us. With this in mind the Spaniards were always referred to as 'our friends.'

From the very beginning of their time on Whiteway, the importance of learning English was emphasised. Another point also stressed and most strongly, was that alcohol was not permitted in the Hall.

Much generosity was shown from those in and around Whiteway. A

Stroud greengrocer sent a gift of oranges and bananas, and donations and fund-raising brought in another £7 9s 8d. Although it appeared to some of the colonists that much of our 'friends'' time and energy was spent lounging about playing the guitar they had brought with them, and luring all the pretty girls in the district from the local lads, this was not really the case.

Some of the time was spent looking for employment. Any money they earned was equally divided between them, with perhaps a small amount being contributed towards their living costs. As time progressed and more income was forthcoming, Bert Mardell was appointed as Work Secretary and the Spaniards agreed to pay twenty percent from their Work Fund towards their keep.

A letter was received from the British Committee, which asked for notification of when work was found before it commenced. Another, from the Spanish Committee to their men, suggested that they might try for work within the National Defence, Hospital or Fire Services. More variety of work became available when the Ministry of Labour decided to allow agricultural work into its repertoire.

Unfortunately this entailed form filling, a difficult task even to those English speakers amongst us, let alone a group of Spaniards, who had only been in the country a matter of a few months. Gallantly Nellie Shaw and Mary Robert volunteered to help out with this particular ordeal.

Nicholas, one of the group who was by profession a cobbler and always in demand, began his work as soon as the appropriate tools could be found for him. Salvador, on the other hand, hoped to find work in Bristol and Basil set about making enquiries in that direction for him. Edwards managed to find employment in a garage in Gloucester and Elesio and Vincent both found work in Gloucester Docks.

Mr Castle from Community House in Gloucester wrote saying that he needed four men on three days a week for three weeks. They would earn six shillings a day plus their bus fares thrown in. Lady Strickland was willing to pay ten pence an hour for gardening work, providing that Mario was sent.

Mrs Mitchell said she was pleased with Emilo's efforts on her garden and a fine job was done on Bert Mardell's chicken run. The wire for it was so deeply embedded into the ground to prevent the chickens from scratching their way out, that even in 1991 some of it still remained, and it was a struggle to get rid of.

Three months after their arrival it was found that most of the refugees had Scabies. The Medical Officer was informed, and the tedious task of disinfecting clothes, bedding and then the entire Hall began.

As the nights drew in and the blackout came into force, it was found that there was a shortage of material suitable to meet the demands of the number of windows in the Hall, and a colour wash was tried instead. When this proved inadequate, Bea Adams contributed some brown paper for the end windows under the veranda, and the Spaniards promised to see that all was blacked out each night. They even volunteered to make a dug-out for the colony's use, which was not accepted, but everyone considered it was a kind offer.

Our friends were provided with land at the front of the hall between the path and the wall to cultivate, and another piece behind the Bakehouse where they produced the most wonderful vegetables.

There were a few problems though which did crop up throughout their stay at Whiteway. Blanco, who had worked previously in night clubs, caused some unrest amongst his fellow countrymen when he visited Cheltenham rather too frequently to see his homosexual friends and missed some of his Scabies treatment, so creating the possibility of re-infection among those who had been cured. He was made to leave and placed elsewhere.

Poor Edwards became ill with malaria in the Autumn, and having spent three weeks recovering in Stroud hospital at their expense, was rather shocked when a letter was sent a month later asking for £1 16s 0d to cover the cost of his keep while he was staying there. The Spaniards volunteered to pay for this unexpected bill, but were very relieved when the British Committee stepped in and offered to cover the cost instead.

There was also the time when Nicholas complained that his tools and work table had been interfered with, and some of his gardening tools had been taken and not returned. Felipe, their secretary was left to sort that one out.

On the whole though, their two years spent on Whiteway were not too disruptive. If the Hall was needed for a function, then they went elsewhere if it was private but, as often as not, joined in with the rest, contributing much by their presence. Sometimes they held a social evening for the colonists where food was cooked by them in the Spanish way, a style of eating about which not a great deal was known in those days before holidays abroad and the package deal. Also, every so often a Ladies Evening would be organised, to which only the Whiteway ladies were invited and made to feel special.

Gradually the numbers of men using the Hall decreased as accommodation was offered locally and employment in London and Gloucester was taken up, or they got married and moved away. Before leaving they organised a show for the colonists as a thank you for all they had done for them.

The Schoolroom remained as living quarters for a few more years after the Spaniards had departed, the first occupant painted part of the outside of the Hall as payment for its use, and the others became caretakers and stayed until 1945.

# *Chapter 16*

# THE SWIMMING POOL

The people of Whiteway had always wanted a pool in which to bathe, a dream which was fulfilled in July 1969. It had taken from as early as August 1912, when George Mackenzie first put his idea to the Colony Meeting, with suggestions of 'a strip being retained by the colony for the purpose of making an open air swimming bath.'

The construction would be a communal effort, with excavated soil removed to shallow areas. It was agreed that a modest size of six yards by thirty yards would be adequate, and not take up too much cultivatable land. Down by the stream was thought to be the most obvious site and Sinclair was asked to join with George in finding and measuring a suitable spot, the results of which would be reported at the meeting in October.

George's suggestion came in the heat of summertime and it sounded idyllic and a simple thing to create. Unfortunately the land considered as suitable by most people was being cultivated by the Kavanaghs who were residing temporarily in the Studio. It would have been inconsiderate to have seized it there and then, at least before they had the benefit of their crops.

When October came around and temperatures, together with the urgency to begin digging, had cooled, no one seemed to mind when the pool idea was shelved. Decisions were made to reserve the land chosen for a future time and commence when the land changed hands. On Mackenzie's departure two years later, his suggestion went with him and was not resurrected for another eleven years.

Colonists were not deprived of somewhere to bathe however, for from its infancy, Whiteway settlers had been in the habit of using the sheep dip when not in normal use. This was situated on the dividing boundary between Causey and colony land, and it has been said how wonderful it was, to be able to lie on the hot stone slabs on the edge, after a dip without clothes on.

When those from outside the Colony heard of these activities, they went out of their way to view the proceedings for themselves, causing the nudism reputation to evolve. Because of this, the habit was discontinued until at the end of the first World War, Stormont Murray gave a series of seven lectures on psycho analysis at a Summer School in July and August, which emphasised how guilt concerning the naked body was an infringement on health and happiness.

*At the sheep dip. A photograph by Hugh van Wadenoyen.*
*L–R: Sue Ryall, Tessa Marin, Janet Ryall.*

Consequently, the sheep dip ritual was revived with relish, and many indulged who would never have considered such a thing before. A few disapproved however and complained. One particular lady tried to get the police to intervene, as she could see nude bodies during her daily excursions to fetch her water from the stream. As the site was hidden from the public road, the police could do nothing, but eventually Sud arranged a bathing rota with no bathing from nine to twelve, and none again from one thirty to seven at night. Anyone who felt impelled to discard their clothes and immerse themselves in water during these hours, was advised to go further along the stream, where they would not be seen.

In 1923, at a summer meeting held at The Bungalow, another enthusiastic gathering discussed the building of a Whiteway bathing pool. They wasted no time in arranging for the digging to commence on the following Saturday. The site chosen on this second occasion was where Sinclair had dug out the clay for his bricks over twenty years before.

The mighty effort that followed was to be short-lived for another important need had arisen and taken all the labour. This was the building of a sturdy road through the Dry Ground, badly needed now that all the extra houses were there.

Exactly a year later, when the road construction effort was in hand but far from completed, the swimming pool digging was resumed, and the cost calculated. It was estimated that £16 10s would be sufficient to complete the project and it could be easily raised if all those interested contributed sixpence a week. Yet again this second digging attempt was forced to grind to a halt, when all effort and money was directed towards the long awaited and much needed Colony Hall and Schoolroom. The money accumulated was loaned to help this latest venture, and a few years passed before it was repaid.

It was the School Group in 1931 who brought up the subject this time, wanting to build a swimming pool for the children. They suggested that it should be situated on the same spot as before, but twelve feet square. Its depth was to be four feet six inches with brick walls, and concrete was to be laid on the bottom. Some members there disagreed with the choice of site, and wished it to go further along the stream. Eventually when no agreement was forthcoming, the meeting broke up, and the whole scheme was abandoned once more.

It was another sixteen years before it was talked of again. On 1 September 1967, Heather White and Pearl Light proposed that 'A swimming pool be erected on the sports ground for the children. The size to be about thirty feet long.' They also added that voluntary subscriptions and social functions would be held to raise the money to fund it.

The site of the old tennis court in the far corner of the field was thought at first to be the best situation, but it was soon considered too far away for safety, and the car park on the opposite corner was chosen instead.

Before jumping in at the deep end, and going the whole hog with the expense and effort of building a solid pool, there was talk of a collapsible one, but most felt that in the end something more permanent was the better bet. Details were discussed, and the safety factor examined. All agreed that to fence it was vital, as was the necessity of some form of continuous supervisial when it was in use.

Additives were essential to purify the water, and in order to learn the whole procedure of pool maintenance, Heather took a short intensive course at Stratford Park Swimming Pool in Stroud. From the information gleaned there, she was able to pass on her knowledge to others who were involved in the daily running. A Swimming Pool Committee was formed, and the whole project, physically and financially, was conducted by them, and continues to be so.

In August the following year, a gymkhana was held on Clay Piece, a field belonging to Mr Dickinson who farmed at Wayside Farm to raise money. This added £40 pounds to the fund. Incredibly by November, £176 had been raised, £50 of which had already been spent. A Christmas Fayre and several jumble sales followed, and as the finances grew, work steadily progressed.

*Whiteway swimming pool today.*
*(Photograph by Katrina Thacker)*

Phil Stewart from the Fostons Ash dug the hole, and miraculously in July 1969, twenty-two months after its initial proposition, it was officially opened with a flood-lit evening swim. The fence agreed upon was erected around it, and the gate at the top fitted with a padlock.

Stringent rules were enforced, for no one wanted an accident. It was decided that an adult was to be there at all times, and no child under the age of sixteen was to swim without supervision. The key was to be held by a member of the Committee, hopefully one who lived nearby, and those wishing to swim had to fetch it, and remain responsible for it until its return. A weekly cleaning rota was introduced, with just routine duties on weekdays, and a grand cleaning effort, with hoovering, back-washing and elsan emptying at the weekend. The year after opening, annual overheads were considered and membership fees fixed.

The pool proved to be extremely successful during its first year and the weather had been warm. A small blue paddling pool for the toddlers was placed in the corner for safety away from the pool's edge, and at weekends

*A gathering at the pool in 1973.*
*Back: Elsie Johnson with grandson Jacob, –?–.*
*Front: Margaret Hawkes, Emma Hawkes, Leanne Williams, Andrew Williams, Jennifer Protheroe with Katrina Thacker, –?–, Frankie Williams, Graham Cook, Teresa White, Debbie Tidy.*

and in the holidays, mothers and children would congregate to swim, talk, and even knit. It united many who having been closeted in their homes during the cold winter months were now able to see their friends again, while their family enjoyed themselves splashing and laughing.

With this increase of people came an increase in noise which particularly affected those who lived nearby, and usually occurred at times when in the past they had peace. Set times of opening were introduced, and the access moved to further down the lane. A changing hut had been one of the earliest amenities introduced with a lavatory to the side. However with the addition of a filtration plant, it was sacrificed to house this humming contraption, together with the chemicals, and cleaning equipment.

In 1990 a screen of conifers was planted around the pool's circumference, and now that they have grown, the pool is completely hidden from view. The cover, purchased a year or so ago, has helped to keep it clean, and very inviting the water looks on a hot summer's day.

The pool has had its troubles, and many people over the years have devoted many hours of their time towards looking after it. Parents have become fed up with being dragged to it continually during hot weather, and it is expensive to maintain, and some folk wonder if it is worth it. George Mackenzie if he were here today to see it, would be pleased and so would all those colonists from the past who longed so much for a bathing pool and never had one.

# *Chapter 17*
# THE LAND TRIBUNAL

The court case held before the Chief Registry Tribunal on 22 November 1955 was a paradox for the Whiteway pioneers' principles of not wanting to be bound by legality. However, the remaining and unbroken communal rule of the holding and administration of colony land was endorsed by the law, when the situation arose of it being put to the test. The result meant that Whiteway Colony would continue for the rest of its life as intended at its establishment. It also proved the strength of community spirit, and that the colonists in 1955 were just as proud of Whiteway and its method of distributing and holding land as the pioneers before them. This pride continues today, and the complicated land allocation system operates now exactly as it has from its formation, allowing the choice of future colonists and admitting only those acceptable to the majority.

Whiteway's conventions were challenged by a lady resident who had lived on Whiteway for many years, coming as a young woman with the man who eventually became her husband. She claimed that she knew nothing of the normal procedure, where a person wishing to live on the colony must apply to the meeting for the land their prospective house stands on, or that on leaving, it must be relinquished.

This seems amazing when every potential colonist has gone, and continues to go, through this necessary formality. It is useless to consider purchasing any dwelling on the land held in the Whiteway system, unless the decision of the meeting, the official governing body of Whiteway, is favourable.

This lady was old, and sadly for her had never integrated with her fellow colonists, or even liked living on Whiteway for the forty-two years she had been there. Her protest against the system proved without doubt that Whiteway land can never be used for personal material gain, and that longevity of landholding or extent of acreage will never make the property on which it stands any more valuable to seller or buyer. In fact, in those days of large plots, sometimes the land was divided once it was back in colony hands. A statement sometimes added to houses advertised in the papers stated 'the land you see is not necessarily the land you'll get'.

At a meeting held thirty years previously in 1925, it had been agreed that when colony land was transferred from one person to another, a meeting should always be called to help the parties concerned, 'to keep alive the bond of unity and common responsibilities, and principle of possession of land for use only.' It was felt by all that land questions should be settled by open discussion in a general gathering of the Colony 'rather than by violence either legal or illegal.' In addition, that all settlers should voluntarily sign the declaration against reversion of Whiteway land into private ownership.

The lady's defiance in ignoring this vital rule, hampered the selling of her house. The prospective buyer, having been warned that the house would never be his if the situation continued, ignored the advice, and installed electricity, and worked the ground on which the house stood regardless. As a result he eventually lost his money, and the lady her buyer.

The outcome of the investigation proved interesting and thought provoking, and one wonders what those who pioneered this colony, pronouncing their freedom with such fervency, would have thought of it all. Only Sud in poor health and now living in Salisbury knew of the situation, but he died shortly afterwards, the outcome possibly hastening his demise.

Incredible though it might seem, the hearing proved that our ancestors had been using a form of ancient land tenure dating from 1200 AD. Further more, it proved that the Colonists as a whole were the licensees of their land, with their important monthly meeting held regularly from its very formation, the licensor.

Consequently the lady's application was dismissed by the Law Court, with the papers publicising the entire affair.

Views came from every angle. *Freedom* commenting on the decision in their issue of 3 December wrote,

> The findings are interesting and enlightening, and however much it may have embarrassed some of the colonists to go to law, they are to be congratulated on the forthright and enthusiastic way they defended a worthy principle . . . It is refreshing when courts are daily filled with people fighting each other over ownership of property, to read of a case in which people are standing up for the right of not owning it.

On their return on the evening of the case, Tom and Gassy were welcomed with the first of two homecoming parties held to celebrate the outcome. The first crammed fifty colonists into the Press Secretary's house, with a second of equal jubilation held a couple of days later when Mary Robert, the Colony Secretary, returned following a stay with a relative in the capital. The concern for mankind and the equality that those who had set up Whiteway felt, had continued to smoulder through the years, taking only a small spark to ignite it into a mighty flame. Their determination

*The surprise home-coming celebration.*

*Back: Tom Keell Wolfe, Gerald Phelps, Sidney Allen, Michael Grendon. Middle: Joy Evans, Winnie Evans, Allen Blackwood, Mick Gilmore, Gassy, Phyllis Allen, Hilda Davis, Hilda Gustin. Bottom: Peter Evans, Dolly Payne, Alan Maxfield, Alan Usher, Jeanne and Lill Smith.*

enabled them to raise the funds with which to fight their cause so enabling the distribution and holding of their land to continue as before.

Most felt sorry for the old lady. Sorry that all those years had passed and she had not felt able to avail herself of the happiness she could have found if she had tried. Their concern was genuinely shown, when instead of completely accepting the ruling of the judge that she should pay the total hearing costs, they let her off, and paid theirs themselves.

Despite all the controversy and speculation regarding Whiteway, it has turned out not to be quite as unconventional as it might seem, for the test case 'proved' the system of Whiteway land holding to be legally acceptable.

The newspapers reported the whole affair, some emphasizing this and others that. Some did hit the nail on the head, the *Daily Mail* wrote

> At a meeting held to report on the proceedings in the Hall on Sunday 27 November, Tom Keell Wolfe told fifty-two colonists, The principles of our founders have been upheld in the London Courts. No-one can sell Colony land – it is the property of every one of us. It cannot pass out of our possession.

The gentleman who had been wanting to buy the house said after the case that he had only wanted the land anyway. Not surprisingly, he decided that Whiteway and its community was not the place for him after all.

The last word goes to *The Citizen* on the Thursday of that momentous week with Gassy's comment which sums the whole affair up,

> I really felt that the old Whiteway was very much alive again. I think last night will remain one of the most unforgettable joys of my life to find the old Whiteway resurrected.

# Chapter 18
# WHITEWAY'S SOCIAL LIFE

The social life of Whiteway has always been important to the Colonists. It is recorded how weekly gatherings were held at Bidfield cottages during the first year, with Mr and Mrs Jolly from Sheepscombe contributing towards poetry and play readings.

Whiteway House, although limited for space, became the centre of entertainment with anything from piano and violin recitals, to talks and Christmas parties, until larger rooms became available at the onset of individual living. Parlour games, such as Charades, Isaac and Rebecca, a game very similar to Blind Man's Buff, Dumb Crambo, Consequences and community singing were all included, with the traditional Family Coach told faithfully by Nellie Shaw every year.

Jeannie with her musical talents, entertained colonists on her piano practically from the moment she arrived. When she moved into Meadow Cottage, her Saturday musical evenings became a regular treat for colonists and visitors, many of whom walked up from Sheepscombe specifically for them. Jeannie played pieces by many composers, her favourites being

*Colonists assembled on Meadow Cottage bank, listening to Jeannie's piano concert.*

Beethoven, Chopin and Grieg. The audience who littered the bank outside her open window, sometimes contributed towards the variety by joining in with their own favourite songs and recitations.

In about 1914, there was an abundance of accomplished players of stringed instruments on the colony, with Kit Hoggett, Allen Blackwood, and John Chamberlain, and they added to the evening also, either individually or as a quartet with Jeannie. When the weather was wet or cold, and listening from outside became impossible, all Jeannie's enthusiasts crowded into her sitting room, sitting closely together on the floor, until there was no more space. Jeannie continued the ritual until 1924, when this form of musical evening came to an end.

Music was then obtained from another source. A gramophone was bought, and a library of records, to suit all tastes was collected. On Wednesday evenings those wishing to hear prominent classical composers were able to indulge themselves in the works of Mozart, Handel and Delius. Thursday evenings were arranged on a Desert Island Disc type format, with a single person selecting their personal favourites each time.

In May 1929, all felt that a new, more modern, type of player was required. An appeal was launched to raise the necessary funding to purchase an electric gramophone and wireless set, priced at £150, but which could be bought for £40 if the record cabinet was excluded. Recitals collected £8 and a bazaar at Whitsun, together with several donations raised some more. By June this modern radiogram was installed in the Hall with running costs estimated at £13 a year, and a committee was formed to look after it, and a gramophone group to support it.

It was in 1924 that the crystal set was introduced to Whiteway. Fred Charles was the first to construct one, closely followed by George Barker, Gus Marin and Jack van Wadenoyen. Three of these incorporated valves into their appliances. By the following year the number of sets on Whiteway had increased to ten.

During the mid 1930's, a change of format in the organisation of Whiteway's social events took place. A club was formed and met, not in the Colony Hall as had become the custom, but at a house built by Hugo van Wadenoyen for himself, but by then sold to Mrs New. This new amenity was for members only who paid 1s 6d a month for its privileges and varied entertainments. These included games such as billiards, darts, cards and dominoes etc on Wednesdays with dances and musical evenings held on Saturdays. There were also film shows, play readings and birthday parties at other times.

A Committee was formed to run the club – with the approval of its members, and although on its formation it was thought that membership would be reasonably small, soon it became so popular, that nearly twenty colonists belonged to it. There were however some colonists who disliked the idea that such a facility should be present on Whiteway, which for all its existence had been free with all its forms of social life. To pay for entertainment was in opposition to their principles. After a transfer to Vivian Lewis's at The Tea Pot, and a general decline in its functions, the club closed down in May 1941, and the Hall became the hub of all Whiteway's social activities once more.

In 1943, cinema shows made their appearance. The first one was held in the Hall in January, with Bert Mardell providing the film, Vivian Lewis the generator, and Bernard Gabbott from the non-Whiteway land, the camera. The same year, at Whitsun, a silent film was shown. Later the Ministry of Information began to give documentary type films, which proved so popular that they were shown regularly each week.

In June 1944, the Hall acquired its own electricity plant, installed by both Vivian Lewis, father and son, solely for lighting and gramophone purposes. The total cost for both plant and the accommodation in which to house it being £49 16s 5d. An electric light and gramophone fund was created to cater for its demands. But in May 1945 Vivian reported that it required better care, for the batteries had been neglected and allowed to run dry, and the engine given too much attention and over oiled. Persons were appointed to render this service.

New settlers introduced their own particular customs alongside those already in existence. Peter and Kate Myllles from Glasgow introduced a social aspect to what otherwise proved to be a boring but necessary chore. They called it 'Sewing Beas'. The women on Whiteway, comparatively few in number in 1904, all convened once a week in a Colonist's house, endeavouring, whilst there, to repair every mendable article for their host in just one sitting. Sometimes, as they sewed, someone read aloud to them, but I suspect that a good gossip was the normal procedure. The following week another lucky colonist had her turn.

Rachelle from the United States brought the American custom of Surprise Parties. The idea was for all colonists to proceed in secret to a new Colonist's house, taking with them a welcoming gift, which they presented to the surprised householder, all of which was followed by a communal picnic. This custom lasted for twenty odd years.

As mentioned before, plays became very important to Whiteway life, and Rachelle's children, Sonia and John, contributed in no small way towards their popularity. They were about ten and twelve years old when they acted out their first play, written entirely by them, and performed in 1905 in Sinclair's newly built cow shed. They followed up their success with more

*Many well known Whiteway faces here, dressed up for one of Whiteway's plays in the twenties.*

*A Whiteway picnic.*

drama productions in succeeding years, even going as far as to produce Edward Carpenter's *St George and the Dragon*.

*The Importance of being Earnest* was performed in George Kenworthy's rick yard, now Hilltop Farm, in 1913 and Bea Adams' lawn became the setting for George Bernard Shaw's, *Press Cuttings*. This play was produced by Nellie Shaw's brother, a professional stage manager in America. Another of Shaw's plays, *You Never Can Tell*, was acted out in The Long Hut, and Mrs Irving's Company from Cheltenham came up in 1927 to entertain colonists to *The Bitter Truth* with recitations and dances in the Workshop. Just a sample of the many and varied entertainments.

Most Sunday afternoons during the summer, a colony picnic was arranged, somewhere away from Whiteway. Dillay woods was a favourite. Each person contributed some item of food which produced a feast of variety, and after the kettle had boiled, and tea had been consumed, games such as rounders were played.

During the wintertime, when snow covered the ground, another type of sport was indulged in on sloping field opposite the Wet Ground. This was of a more individual kind, requiring a sledge. Sledging continues each year on this field, the only difference being that large plastic bags are now available for use.

Gassy recalls how once in 1918, the bakehouse van was used to convey sleeping necessities, and ample food to nourish those who took part in a night picnic, held by a haystack below Honeycombe Farm.

Communal teas and picnics have always been regular features at Whiteway, for even after hard physical work on some combined colony scheme, there always seemed to be enough energy left to follow up with a communal picnic.

The 30 October 1948 was an important date as it brought Whiteway's Golden Jubilee. An exhibition of old Whiteway photographs, with artifacts produced by our craftsmen was set up in the Hall. Some were there actually demonstrating their skills, Flossie Davies with her spinning wheel and Rene Adams weaving on her loom. There was cabinet work from Fred Foster, and book binding by Basil Robert, sandal making by Stanley Randolph and Dr Margenout's embroidery work. Douglas White was there demonstrating his engine models, one of which had the power to transport up to five children in one go. There was also produce from the bees and the garden.

An enormous cake weighing 25 lbs and adorned with 50 candles was provided by Protheroe's Bakery. When the evening came, there was a social with games and a display of folk dancing. At one stage of the evening all the children born on Whiteway were asked to stand together in the centre of the hall, and many were surprised to see what a large group they made.

*Whiteway's 50th anniversary. Jeannie Protheroe and Bea Adams with Protheroe's cake.*

When ten o'clock came, the giant bonfire which had been assembled outside the Hall was lit, and mock deeds thrown into its flames by Bea Adams.

The celebrations continued the following day when the exhibition was reopened, and the afternoon's special event of planting a commemorative copper beech tree, known as the Jubilee Tree took place amid the ashes from the previous evening's bonfire. Bea once again in her capacity as the oldest colonist bar one, the other being Jeannie Protheroe unable to be there that day, ceremonially assisted in this emotional event. Meanwhile the younger members of the colony continued to enjoy their involvement in the festivities with a party specially arranged for them in the schoolroom.

Past memories had been resurrected, old acquaintances renewed, and all felt the unity of the village where many present had spent so many years of their lives.

The following year Whiteway and District Sports Day was held on Bank Holiday Monday, being opened by Ben Parkin MP at one o'clock. There were races of varying lengths, tug of war and cycle races. Side shows and refreshments, not to mention lucky number programmes were available, all

*Some of those at the Jubilee.*
*L–R: Lottice Davies, Doolie (Priscilla Ashdown), Kay Ellis, Winnie and Rene Adams, Joy Evans, Jo Mardell, Deirdre Blackwood.*

at the cost of 1s for adults and 6d for children. This became an annual event for several years with flowers and produce being introduced the following year. It was held on Clay Piece belonging to Mr Dickinson until 1952, when Whiteway's own field was available for this event for the first time. A new Sports and Social Club was started, replacing the old one begun in 1948, and Mr Dickinson and his family invited to attend as guests as an expression of gratitude for all the years he had allowed his field to be available for Whiteway's use. There were sixteen fund raising events on the programme, and following a successful day, the whole thing was rounded off with a dance and ballet display in the evening.

In June 1952 Doris and Mick Gilmore, both Londoners, bought Bea Adams' bungalow. They had visited Whiteway for holidays for many years, staying at Lambda, The Tea Pot, The Bungalow and DOP next door. It was while they were at DOP that they were informed that The Bungalow was for sale. Doris and their son Jeff moved in on 1 April 1953, with Mick following later, after sorting out his working arrangements.

Doris loves children, and welcomed the colony's children to her house on

*Playing some sort of game. Could that be a cricket bat?*

a Sunday afternoon, when there would be a get-together. She undertook the running of the Miserden cubs for a while, until its closure when numbers dropped to two. Every fortnight Mick and Doris would hold whist drives at their home, which proved so popular that as many as sixteen people would turn up, bringing food, and turning the whole thing into a party.

Then, in 1954, Richard and Ann Wolfe asked Mick if he would help then start a new Youth Club. There had been a similar club in 1947 called the Whiteway and District Youth Club, which met mainly on Sunday afternoons in the Schoolroom. This had been successful, especially with their performance of *A Midsummer Night's Dream* on Bea Adams' lawn in June 1947, but had since died out, and another one was required.

Mick agreed to help, and another Whiteway Youth Club was formed. Mick had been a PT Instructor in the Navy, having qualified in his spare time at Tooley Street when only seventeen years of age. He had also taught physical training in the Boy's Brigade, so he was well equipped for such a task.

The Club met twice a week on Tuesdays and Thursdays, and as they had no equipment, Mick would take a football to the Hall, and they would all play ground ball with that. There was a need to raise money, and this was achieved mainly through subscriptions. The remainder was earned, given, begged, or raised by some fund raising event.

As their fame grew, the club attracted about forty youngsters from Whiteway, Miserden, Camp, Stroud and even Cheltenham. Each member contributed whatever they could afford towards the Club funds, and if they genuinely could not afford anything, they were let off.

Another fund for records was also in operation, into which each member contributed sixpence a week. When enough money had accumulated a joint decision was made as to which record would be purchased. The radiogram was boxed in a cabinet which included space to accommodate the ever growing record collection, and Mick acquired a set of wall speakers from a friend who was a disc jockey.

It was a peaceful club, and during its ten year existence, Mick had only one member who had to be asked to leave. If any damage occurred, which sometimes happened, with such large numbers regularly involved, then the materials had to be purchased and the damage repaired by the culprit. When completed, it would be examined and a decision made on how much they should contribute towards the total cost.

Once during a Colony Meeting, there was rather a lot of noise coming from the rear of the hall, and someone enquired as to what it was, only to be informed that it was a couple of the Youth Club members mending a window which they had broken. As time passed the equipment owned by the Youth Club became something to be proud of.

There was a three-quarter billiard table, two dart boards, a skittle alley, three table tennis tables and two additional portable pool tables. The billiard table cost £7 10s 0d, including cues, balls and scoring boards and came from Hucclecote near Gloucester. Collecting it was no easy task, for the room in which it was housed was on the second floor, and anyone knows that negotiating stairs with heavy slabs of slate is not the easiest task in the world.

Frank Finch provided the lorry and additional necessary labour, and on its safe arrival at Whiteway, the whole laborious process was repeated, until the table was standing proudly in its new abode in the Schoolroom. There it remained, and no-one ever attempted to remove or steal it. Basil Robert regularly came down to the Club evenings, specifically to teach the youngsters the techniques of billiard playing.

Mick and his Youth Club ran jumble sales, dances and countless other events. The Bonfire Night celebrations were organised for many years by them. They undertook the house-to-house money collections which contributed towards the cost of the fireworks, and amassed the wood for building the fire. During the preceding weeks, colonists would send word if they had anything for the fire and offerings would be taken to where they eventually formed an enormous pile. This was, and still is, situated on the grassy triangle of land towards the front of the Hall.

In the Youth Club days, Pat Elliott would be given the collected money together with a donation from the Club, and purchase a suitable selection of fireworks from a wholesalers in Gloucester. One year someone else was allotted this task, and bought mainly bangers, so he never got the job again.

At 6.30 on the night itself, colonists, friends, and previous members of the Colony, not to mention countless children, bobble hats on their heads and boots on their feet, gathered under the verandah in front of the Hall. Excitement was in the air. The fire was lit and with encouragement from a gallon or two of paraffin or sump oil roared into life. Inevitably the wind would be blowing well towards the Hall together with showers of sparks, which always introduced the fear that the Hall and everything within range of this inferno, would surely go up in flames.

The tantalising aroma of sausages and fried onions which had been wafting through the atmosphere for at least the last half hour, now materialized into an edible form. Even those who had partaken of their tea just a short while before were able to find enough extra space to accommodate a hot dog, or possibly two, after which it was time for the fireworks to have their turn. Catherine wheels on posts rotated at speed, or disappointingly remained where they were, and rockets shot into the air, amid 'oohs and aahs'.

Sometimes the very tiny tots were able to hold a sparkler just for themselves, or their brother or sister did it for them if they were a little bothered. When food and fun was over, all trudged home, reeking of smoke and bloated with food.

The following morning, the still smouldering fire was attended once more, with those who went with intention of clearing it up, rekindling it once more with the addition of leftover partly burnt remains. These helpers enjoyed their Sunday morning, almost as much as the Saturday night.

During the years of the Whiteway Youth Club everyone would, in some way or another, end up at Mick and Doris' house on Christmas Eve, even if they had made arrangements to be elsewhere for the earlier part of the evening. There would be food and drink available and all were content to listen to records or simply sit and talk. In fact this was not always confined to that particular day, but seemed to often spread over to the New Year.

On the Club's closure, which to Mick seemed the most sensible thing to do at the time, as the majority of members then were from outside districts, there was £30 in the fund. This was given to the Colony, to be used in the future by anyone else who wished to begin such a scheme. The billiard table remained in the schoolroom for some years after, available for those who

*Mike Hawkes at work in the studio at his home, which he shares with his artist wife Margaret.*

wished to use it. Eventually it was put under the floor, when the space was required for other purposes.

I am sure on reading this, many people around the forty- to fifty-year age group will have memories of the Whiteway Youth Club, and all they did while members.

Doris was still to be involved with children in 1973, when there were nearly a dozen little pre-school-age children on Whiteway who needed occupation. She with 'Daisy May', her friend who lived opposite, ran the newly-formed Whiteway Playgroup in association with the mothers, for two years, until it got on its feet, always being always present, while the mothers helped out on a rota basis.

Fund raising, for even that was like the other times in Whiteway history, was of a social nature with bonfires and communal singing, wine and cheese parties under the trees with tilly lamps and just-for-fun picnics down in the woods.

In November 1970, with several youngsters on Whiteway under fifteen years needing an energetic way in which to let off steam Mike Hawkes, a pictorial pub sign artist and recent resident on Whiteway formed Whiteway Wanderers, a non-league football team of which he was both manager and coach. He lived at the Red House which became Red Roofs and then Hazeldene.

The team comprised an assortment of lads from Whiteway, Miserden and Edgeworth. Games were played at home and away in the surrounding villages. The first game played on Whiteway Sports Ground was against Uplands, with the grass just recently cut and still lying on the ground. Stan Johnson made the goal posts and one of the team designed the badge, which, it was not discovered until much later was really the authentic logo of Wolverhampton Wanderers, the initials being the same and thus suiting both teams. With a drop in the number of members of suitable age Mike wound up his club in the early eighties.

## *Chapter 19*

# THE FAMILIES OF WHITEWAY

The third generation of Whiteway colonists came in the thirties, forties and fifties, some of whom were direct descendants of those settlers from the early years. They have remained living on Whiteway, and today have children and in several cases grandchildren.

The Adams' family is such an example. Bert Mardell came to Whiteway in 1926 living in The Red House with his first wife Alice, from whom he subsequently split. He formed a union with Rene, and they lived in Rose Cottage where their two daughters, Josephine and Madeline, were born. After moving to Letchworth and Rugby they returned to Whiteway in about 1936 to take up residence in Nooitgedacht, the Dutch for 'I would never have believed it!'. The name was very apt in this situation, for it was an old GWR waggon brought to Whiteway from Swindon in 1924 by Hugo Van Wadenoyen, a Dutchman from Cardiff, who became renowned far and wide for his photography.

He had it transported to Whiteway by lorry, and assisted by practically all the men of the Colony, manoeuvred it via ropes and levers, over to a hole which had been dug in 1918 when the search was on for hard-core for a

*The Train.*

future Colony hall. Hugo shared this unique home with his brother Jackot, his wife Jessica and their son 'Little Hugo' intermittently, until they were there so infrequently that they were asked in 1946 to relinquish their land. This meant that Rene and Bert who had stayed in the carriage and worked the land in their absence for well over eight years, could officially take it over.

The interior of the waggon was always warm, probably due to the close fitting doors and windows. The two end sections, which formed Rene and Bert's bedroom and the kitchen, added by Hugo, were cooler. The central portion, the main body of the carriage, had a small extension at the back, where a writing desk stood. It was also equipped with a small fireplace with an asbestos piping chimney. This fireplace had a small oven to its side, which was never used to cook on, although as it was permanently warm, it proved invaluable for the incubation of Bert's young chicks. All the cooking was done on a primus stove. Rene did all the decorating, and wove the material from which the curtains were made. The weekly bath was taken at The Bungalow, where Bea had an upstairs bathroom, and a small range in the kitchen which was stoked up especially on Sundays when baths were taken in preparation for the week ahead. For daily requirements, they used a washbasin in their bedrooms. The waggon also had a cellar which was reached from the outside down a rocky path.

Their second daughter Madeline who, as a child, spent six years from 1940–46 in hospital, used to lie flat on her back, when allowed home, on the built up patio at the front of the carriage which proved to be a lovely suntrap. She had a wheelchair which enabled her to be mobile and someone took her out every afternoon. She laughs when she recalls how she was transported between the waggon and the wheelchair in a wheelbarrow, which was parked above the slope in readiness for her. Once when this transfer was taking place, the wheeelbarrow tipped over, and she fell out and rolled down the bank.

As it was thought that fresh air would aid her recovery, Madeline slept out in one of Bea's garden sheds with a paraffin stove to provide heat in the winter. The shed was her bedroom until she left home in 1952, to live in Gloucester.

The children would often visit Mrs Mitchell, who lived just down the lane. She lived in the Cloisters, probably so called because her daughter was a nun, and was always referred to by the Mardell children as the 'The Princess'. She gained this delightful name because she always dressed beautifully and was kind to them. She once gave Madeline a set of yellow beads, which she still has in her possession today.

In 1946, Ted Adams died unexpectedly in his sleep. The Mardell family

*The Cloisters and the Wet Ground Road. The house began as a hut brought from Walthamstow by Will Stevens in 1911.*

moved up to the Bungalow to be with Bea. There they had not only a bedroom upstairs, but a further two downstairs and two toilets outside in the garage, one at each end.

Half of the Workshop meanwhile, the part nearest the road, was converted into a home for the Mardells, with a kitchen facing the road and two bedrooms behind it. One of these was converted to a bathroom during the sixties. Later Patrick Elliott's half, where he had lived as a bachelor, was incorporated into their living space with a large lounge, devoid of a ceiling, completely open to the rafters.

Madeline can remember that when they took it over the stage, which had formerly been used for plays, was still in the corner with big heavy curtains around it. It was in there that she kept her white mice. A fire was installed in this room though with little chance of keeping it warm until finally, in the 1970s, a ceiling was put in, along with additional heating in the form of storage heaters. The kitchen on the other hand was always warm and inevitably most used.

Jack Van Wadenoyen was asked to remove the train when it was no longer used, but on his failure to do so, it was demolished by Bert and Alan Pope, after Stroud District Council had pronounced adverse feelings on its presence.

Bea meanwhile, who suffered from severe arthritis, continued to live in The Bungalow for several more years, until her condition deteriorated to such an extent that full-time nursing was required. She moved to another colony house, Whitehaven, where she was cared for until her death in 1954. On her departure from The Bungalow, the land she had held there was divided, with Rene and Bert acquiring over an acre more, to add to their existing plot.

Rene still worked her loom when she was able. She weaved the material for her lounge curtains, table runners, and even Bert's suits, the fabric for which, when completed, was taken to a tailoress in Stroud who transformed it into suits. Jo can remember, at the time of her departure to college in 1949, Rene thought that a suit was the right thing to wear, so the material was woven, and a tailoress employed to fit and make the outfit.

On the occasion of Madeline's marriage, to make more room available for the reception, the loom was removed from its customary position in the lounge, and hidden in the hall behind an enormous cavernous wardrobe. Later it was transferred to the attic where, a few years later when woodworm was discovered, it was banished from the house. A sensible precaution when a building is constructed entirely from wood! The looms remains were last seen in one of the Nissan huts.

Bert had erected the two Nissan huts after the War to accommodate his flock of hens, which hitherto had been housed in several chicken houses and runs, scattered over a large expanse of his ground. The eggs collected from these twice daily, were wiped and placed on trays holding two and a half dozen each, before being packed into boxes, and stacked in the hall of the workshop. They were then taken to Cheltenham where the little 'lion' mark, denoting approved quality was stamped on each one, before being distributed to shops to be sold. Geese were kept at one time, but the children were frightened of them, and would not go down the garden when they were there.

Judith travelled to school in Stroud by bus, the cost being seven pence in old money. If it snowed during the school day, pupils from the Whiteway area were always allowed to go home early, as the roads in this vicinity are renowned for getting blocked by the drifting snow. Often times they could be totally impassable, with no chance of breaking through until the snow plough came. The surrounding fields would remain practically clear, most of their snow from them having been blown onto the road by the wind. With this in mind snow fencing is now erected in an attempt to prevent it.

The two most memorable winters of the century were those of 1948 and 1963. All was well at Christmas, 1962, until the afternoon of Boxing Day. Many of us can remember the first scattering of snow that day and the 'Christmassy' feeling that accompanied it. The following day a huge expanse of deep white snow covered the country, deceiving everyone with its beauty,

*Snow at Whiteway in 1947.*

and giving no indication of the chaos and turmoil that it would bring during the next three months.

Whiteway, together with many other villages, was completely cut off, and remained so for the following fortnight. Three cars were buried between Highfields at the entrance to the Colony and Wateredge, the farm at end of the road. The bakery, which was unable to deliver its normal quota of bread and cakes was forced to reduce its output. Although Whiteway itself was fortunate to have a supply on its very doorstep, the shop's stock was gradually depleted until it was necessary to obtain more, by some means or another.

Many colonists had to dig themselves out through the Colony lanes with shovels, to clear the road for others to get out with the Bakery van. This venture was undertaken by six enthusiastic youngsters who, unable to go to work, but willing to risk life and limb to get to the wholesalers, dug themselves out as far as Blue Barn. With much pushing and heaving, they managed to accomplish their mission, returning home with their bounty. Judy thinks Steve Merrett was the driver, and recalls how the back of the van was dented on their return, from all the pushing involved every time they got stuck.

No bus was able to get to Whiteway before March because the road leading into the village was so narrow. Even after the snow blower had blasted its way through, allowing access once again to civilization, the build-up of snow either side was so steep that the whole stretch resembled a tunnel and it was much too narrow for anything as wide as a bus to attempt. Therefore, anyone wishing to use public transport to get to Cheltenham or Stroud was required to walk to the Salt Box or the Fostons Ash public house.

Alternatively in the Summer, Judith can remember playing at the sheep dip for hours when she was small, catching tadpoles. When she was older, she played Monopoly, or went go-carting down the lane from their home, a pursuit best not attempted today, with the increase in traffic.

The Mardells did have a car however, inherited from Rene's father. It was an Austin Seven, and even though Judy finds it hard to remember the number of the car she owns today, she has no trouble whatsoever remembering the number of that particular one from all those years ago. It was AAD 385. This recollection is partly influenced by a suitcase in her bedroom. As the luggage rack was at the back of their car, which when loaded up obliterated the number plate, one of the suitcases had the licence number written in white on its side.

Judy, in the old tradition of Whiteway, built her house herself, gradually over a period of time, on part of her parents' plot. Judy with her husband Bob, and her family are still resident on Whiteway.

*Judith Mardell clearing the ground in readiness for her bungalow in 1965.*

Another family who came in 1922 and whose descendants still live here are the Robert family, and we have already learned how Mary and Basil came from Holt to be part of the Cotswold Co-operative Handicrafts Guild. After their split, Basil and Mary continued working at their craft full time in their newly built workshop, assisted by Andree Griffiths, Nellie Morand and Dennis Light, until 1932 when his craft ceased to be his only source of income, for he took on the post of Rural Industries Organiser, for Gloucestershire Community Council. The Rural Development Commission was set up in response to endeavours by the Women's Institute and other rural organisations to help those living in areas where traditional crafts such as thatching, spinning and weaving, furniture making, the trade of the blacksmith, etc needed promotion. They also provided instruction in modern techniques and gave assistance with growth and sales. The Commission endeavoured to find a market for their goods through exhibitions and advertising, and assisted them in producing a saleable product.

After the War, the Rural Industries Bureaux worked through organisations which were appointed locally by the Rural Community Council. Basil was the chief organiser in three counties, Gloucestershire, Herefordshire and Worcestershire. His work mainly involved helping trades in his area recover after the War and to get the industries going again. Whereas previously blacksmiths had been involved mainly with horses and their attendant equipment, now tractors were increasing and welding was becoming more commonplace. People were encouraged to adapt their skills to cater to the transforming country scene, and produce items accordingly.

Peter, Joy's husband and brother to John and Eulalia Evans, all of whom had spent a large portion of their childhood on Whiteway at their Aunt Kitty's, assisted Basil as number three organiser for a short while, dealing chiefly with Worcestershire. He was mainly concerned with the itinerary of craft instruction, and the founding of the Master Thatcher's organisation. Gloucestershire, Herefordshire and Worcestershire had a high proportion of crafts people then. Whereas other counties would be able to manage with one organiser, three were needed here. However, on feeling the need to produce things himself, instead of advising others who did, he and Joy with baby Rosalind spent a year on the Herefordshire/Wales border, learning furniture making instead.

Joy, as a child, attended The Forest School in Hampshire, a small progressive school, which was non-denominational and non-political. The running of the school was based on the theory that people should learn through nature, seeking the simplicity, good sense and fortitude that it offered, to enhance through its chivalrous spirit, an understanding in daily

*Worcestershire Guild of Designer Craftsmen Exhibition 1991, at Avoncroft Museum of Ancient Buildings.*

life of all peoples. After six years she transferred to the Wynstone's Rudolph Steiner School, which she left at the age of eighteen and a half. She then trained as a nurse at the Royal Free Hospital in London, putting her training to use later when she worked at the Cotswold Sanatorium at Cranham.

When she found she was expecting her second child, Alan, she left, remaining at home until both children began secondary school. During the latter part of the fifties she was able, with more time available, to begin carving, utilizing some of the pieces left over from Peter's furniture making. She produced dishes in the shape of leaves such as oak and maple, but her main pleasure is in deep-relief and three-dimensional carving.

In 1992, when I visited her, she had carved wooden embellishments to a staircase. The acorn sits on the post at the bottom while an owl, a squirrel and a snail occupy other areas of the handrail. Peter has always produced good quality individually made furniture. He prefers if possible to use solid wood in the production of his furniture even though some very good quality veneered products are now on the market and widely available.

Life was hard when he started out, for his craft was not so fashionable then as it has become over the last ten years. He had no machinery to assist in his labour initially, but eventually bought a circular saw to relieve some of the physical work. Now he has more equipment to help with the heavy

*Joy carving.*

*Carved in oak by Joy. A collection bowl at Sapperton Church.*

*Peter in his workshop.*
*(Photograph by Katrina Thacker)*

*An oak chest. One of Peter's many fine pieces of furniture. Photograph by Alan Evans.*

work but the main quality, which no machinery can achieve, is that of design and skill. He makes mainly domestic furniture, and sells to a wide range of people, who want to own something of quality which benefits from use.

The house that Peter and Joy live in was formerly Basil's workshop. When it was no longer used regularly for his craft, it was taken over for a variety of purposes. The County Library used it, and colonists were able to change their books there, not to mention the telephone and the Wardens during the War.

In 1947 Joy and Peter moved in there to live, even though Peter was using it as his workshop at the same time. Gradually they enlarged and altered it and still continue in residence today.

The craft tradition carries on through their son Alan, whose skills we have mentioned before. His workshop stands beside that of his father. He is unable to live on Whiteway at present, but likes to think that one day he will. Rosalind, his sister, lives just a stones throw away from her parents' home. Nevertheless, it is rather comforting to know that three generations of this family have practiced their skills, albeit different ones, all within a few yards of each other.

*Jennifer, Sudbury Protheroe's grand-daughter retains the family link.*

*Greenmeads built by Alf Ryall in 1926. Replaced in 1990.*

*The Ryall family.*
*Back: Rose and Alfred with daughter Sue.*
*Front: Harry Adams, Rose's father with a young visitor Robert Thorndale.*

*Some of the White family who came to Whiteway in 1924. They lived intermittently at The Long Hut and Tinpenny Cottage before settling down at Bidwell in 1946 where they stayed for 21 years. Carl and his family represent them here today. L–R: Lily (Kay) White, Joan Frampton, Chris Palmer and Eva White with handbag.*

*Some more members of the Evans Family.*
*Joy Evans with Winnie Evans (sister-in-law), Rosalind Evans with cousin Sally Evans (kneeling), and John Evans.*

*Leonie Blackwood.*

*Leonie's home Panelis. The name is a combination of Pan (Edward Smith) and Elisa his Swedish wife, old friends of Whiteway. They took over the bottom half of Sud's garden before Allen Blackwood, but left it unbuilt on. (Photograph by Keith Thacker)*

These families are by no means exceptional, for several other old established families are also still here. Apart from the rest of the Evans family, the Protheroes, the Lights, the Palmers and the Maxfields must all be included. Also the Whites who came in 1924, leaving for a while but then returning, the Allens with George's daughter-in-law Amy who married his son Paul, and until recently the Blackwoods with Leonie. You will remember that she was the first baby to be born in Whiteway House. Added to these are the Ryalls with Rose who came with Alf in 1927, and the Tidys, Jonathon's mother Winnie spending much time here as a child, being Jeannie Straughan's niece. Later she too became an Evans on her marriage to John.

All this just goes to prove that having once lived here, those who find it suits them are reluctant to live anywhere else, and those who have left feel drawn to return when they can.

# *Chapter 20*

# A Newcomer's View of Whiteway in the 1960's

What do people see when they come to Whiteway and what impressions do they have of this village upon the hill top? What convinces them that this is the place for them? How and why did the emphasis change from the previous Whitewayans focus on land issues, to that of the present day occupants of Whiteway houses who must be concerned with their property and its value?

I have observed this transition throughout my time here, and have seen how land and house must both be considered by the newcomer. How then do they feel about the somewhat lengthy and unusual procedure of gaining the land upon which the house they are purchasing stands?

All of these questions can be answered only from my own observations, as a newcomer in 1968, who had heard of Whiteway Colony, but was not sufficiently interested to have bothered finding out where it was. How then did we ever end up here, living contentedly, with no wish to move elsewhere?

We wanted to buy a house to renovate, in the country and with a garden. Mrs Inman, the elderly lady to whom our one bedroomed chalet bungalow belonged, wished to move 'before another winter came' and 'without the fuss of people tramping through the house.' My father, a coal haulier who supplied her annual coal delivery, gleaned this information over two strong cups of tea and a buttered scone. Conveying the message to my fiancé and myself, by now wearying of inspecting run down cottages, with underwater streams and sitting tenants, we arranged to visit Mrs Inman and Whiteway Colony.

We arrived on a wet chilly Easter Monday, after consulting a pencil drawn map of the area, sketched on the back of a brown envelope. This was the first time I had stepped on Colony ground, and the impression I received was one of dripping. Everywhere seemed to be surrounded by trees hung with droplets of water and long wet grass brushed our legs as we walked through the gateway, devoid of a gate which was propped against the scrubby trees that grew to the left.

The concrete path which approached the bungalow ran parallel to its boundary hedge and was so prized by Mr Inman who had laid it several

*A view of Whiteway from the air, about 1940. The fields, partly occupied by the Colony, have names from years past. They are Little Meadow, Fish pond Piece which is the land in the sheep dip area, Clay Piece, and Burnt Piece, where the non-Whiteway houses are accommodated. The Mushroom Field was part of Causeys ground.*

years previously, that he refused to allow it to be dug up to accommodate the water pipe to his house, when the colony had acquired its water supply in 1948. A joint supply with Runnymede next door was agreed upon instead, a decision which was to cause problems during the years ahead. Across the front door hung brightly coloured strips of canvas, which were popular then presumably to protect those inside the house from prying eyes, if the weather was hot and they chose to leave their door open, although not really necessary for this bungalow with its large expanse of lawn down to the lane.

Inside it felt cold, but only for a short while, for soon Mrs Inman had lit her boiler in the kitchen, and kindled the wood in her sitting room grate, enabling us to feel the benefit of her five central heating radiators. The remainder of the house was primitive, with no bathroom, toilet, hot water system, or septic tank. Yet here it was with full central heating, a luxury just being introduced into modern estates.

Throughout that summer we visited several times, not entirely decided, and still doing the rounds of properties in the estate agents' hands. But as time rolled on and our visits became more frequent we began to feel a sense of contentment, a quality which remains with us today. On hot days I can remember so well the heat of the sun, as we wandered around the garden with the old lady, who was frail to the eye but physically as strong as an ox. We were now familiar with the land holding process, but this did not deter us, and our final decision to buy the house was an easy one.

On the Thursday evening in September when the cheque had been paid, and the legalities were over, we secured our key and with a few essentials, moved in. They were deliberately sparse, for we intended to improve our home room by room, sleeping in rooms in turn, while the others were in chaos. The old Elsan toilet was removed within five minutes of stepping over the threshhold. It was replaced by a blue plastic bucket with a lid, which had been a wedding present, and proved invaluable for the following two years.

It suited our needs perfectly until we had installed our septic tank and proper lavatory, when a simple ceremony was held to celebrate the occasion.

The daily early morning ritual when the bucket with its contents travelled fervently down the back path, hopefully out of sight of the nearest neighbour, to the hole specially excavated for the purpose of regular refilling was dispensed with, and so was the nightly task of knocking the snow off the lid and brim in winter. The reason for this unusual practice was because I thought it more hygienic and easier on the atmosphere to place it outside the low window at the rear of the bungalow on some old car tyres, opening the window and lifting it in as required, after which any feeling of drowsiness completely vanished.

With no hot water system, an old pottery sink and a tap, which when turned on the first night issued green slime and wriggly worms, made all the worse because I was cleaning my teeth at the time, gave us the impression of stepping back in time by twenty years.

We were in no way unique in this situation however, for many Whiteway houses still had no toilet or bathroom, even long after we had gained ours.

As new young blood we were made particularly welcome, with a present of newly dug potatoes here or some runner beans there. On the birth of our first daughter, Rene Mardell made two nighties and a beautiful smocked silk dress for her, all stitched by hand. Soon after our arrival others of our generation came to join us, as those older ones on Whiteway felt the need for care elsewhere, or simply died.

The houses in 1968 were still comparatively small, many built of wood, but with a scattering of flat-roofed cement-type sectional houses. From the outside some appeared to be in need of a little love and care, but the interiors were surprisingly cosy and spacious, each one different from its neighbour. The houses were an expression of the people inhabiting them. Enclosed by those dripping trees, the result of a tree planting scheme in 1928, lie sixty-eight buildings – a surprise to most visitors. Many houses now have hedges, walls and fences around them, but this has not always been the case, for as all land is jointly held, then boundaries seemed pointless.

Our land had nothing to separate us from our neighbours below, the whole merging as one down to a small pond. Today there is a substantial hedge there but it is not planted as a dividing block to erase those beside us from our view, it was simply because of the fear that my toddling youngster would toddle too far one day, and end up toppling into the pond, now excavated into a beautiful, but deep and dangerous lake.

In earlier times the two fields upon which Whiteway stands had gates, which it was possible to close if required. But now, with the advent of the car, and most living on Whiteway own one or two, the gateways have been widened to accommodate them, and the gates are no more. There was a tradition in years gone by, that all the entrance gates were closed once a year on Good Friday, just to prove that Whiteway land was private, but now we just have signs. All cars here on Whiteway are supposed to be parked on the land of the holder, never on the roads. The main reason for this is because the lanes are so narrow that in an emergency it would be disastrous if the vehicle sent to cope with a situation was unable to get through.

Our roads are bumpy and pot-holed. They are continually an issue of complaint, but they are typical country lanes, unlit by street lamps, a perfect blend with rural life. Some children do not know what it is to walk in total darkness, to be aware of the universe and blackness and sounds of the night.

Their eyes can not take it and their ears are too full of sound.

Everyone who lives on Whiteway has bought his house with a cash sum. How an individual achieves this is his concern, but the result remains the same, for there are no mortgage facilities on Whiteway properties. Also alas, no improvement grants are available even for bathrooms, unless the council has revised its policies recently. This combination of financial pressures, early in the life of a new Whiteway settler, means that the new owners struggle to raise even more money in order to improve their purchases.

We need to return to those early days to see how the policies adopted changed to create the situation we see today. The early settlers applied for a piece of land for cultivation. They invariably erected upon it some movable type of dwelling, constructed of wood or anything that was available and light on the pocket. Value was not of primary importance, for it was not considered a lifelong investment, but a small haven to which they could escape from city and pressures.

The ideal from the early Whitewayans viewpoint was where all possessions of the user-occupier would be cleared from his allotted land when he vacated it, so leaving it clear for his successor. George Allen is the perfect example of this policy, for he removed everything from his ground, transporting it lock, stock and barrel to Herefordshire. Most of those who left invariably let their huts remain, accepting a suitable but modest sum for them from those new occupiers of their land, plus a small extra for any trees or crops incorporated by them whilst they lived there.

This allowed even the lowly to aspire to their wish for involvement in the lifestyle that Whiteway Colony had to offer. For several decades this system worked quite adequately and a constant flow of young and old came and went. The transfer of land being little affected by the addition of living quarters. Those colony children growing up into adults here, were able to apply for part of their parents' large plots which, if granted to them, were measured and divided, still leaving large gardens for all.

Then houses became of vital importance financially to the population as a whole. They became assets. It became important to own your own home. You were encouraged to cosset and enlarge it, furnish and nurture it, in fact pour money into it, for with an item as valuable as this tucked under your belt, security was yours and you were safe. So houses in general became big business.

Those modest Whiteway huts did not entirely escape this modern attitude. Having been purchased, many do-it-yourself enthusiasts visited the newly opened stores which catered for the influx of 'improvers' and they too set about to restoring, rebuilding, and extending their 'investment' as advised. Our home is a perfect example of this. In consequence, the

*Keith doing the work himself, as so many do on Whiteway. With all the stone here, it seems incredible that many older Whiteway houses have cellars. The labour involved must have been tremendous.*

majority of homes on Whiteway today cannot be taken away, although it is true to say that some here are practically as they were when newly built.

Therefore if the owner who has worked and spent time and resources on his home wished to leave the Colony, he expects and needs, if he is buying a property elsewhere, to get a reasonable return on his 'investment.' How else would he be able to afford another? The question we now consider is who, these days, can afford to pay outright for a large house, as opposed to the early years when newcomers bought small huts from settlers to enlarge for their own comfort?

Will the time arrive when the only people who can come here are those with a substantial readily available lump sum? Who now, and in the future, will be in this enviable position? This sadly means that whereas Whiteway was a place where those of all denominations could aspire, as envisaged by Tolstoy, I am afraid that it will soon only be possible for those more fortunate who can afford it, but caring little about its origins.

Alternatively, if you are content to remain on Whiteway, as most here are, then this situation has no significance whatsoever. For those occupants of colony land, however grand or humble their home might be, or whether their status in the eyes of the world is high or low, the common way in which we all hold our land is a marvellous unifier.

This land holding system has remained unchanged from when it came into operation on the Colony's formation. The equality craved by those early socialist settlers has survived completely because of it, and will never change. We could realistically exclude those who are thought to be undesirable, for everyone who wishes to come still applies for their land, whether affluent or otherwise, at least, money in this situation has no influence. Wouldn't those no-money users from that first year, particularly Arnold Eiloart, be delighted to see this, were they still alive.

The land, in my view is better attended today than twenty years ago, perhaps this is because gardening has become a leisure activity. Old Whitewayans might say that flowers were unimportant compared with the need for vegetables and livestock which kept body and soul together, but that was probably a countrywide feeling following the wars anyway.

One of the most attractive aspects of this village is the variety in the gardens, with some quite wild still, filled with secret hideaways. Then there are others which are open stretches of mown grass, neat and organised, filled with masses of vegetables and soft fruits.

The fields surround us, not always quiet as one might think the countryside should be, but full of activity, especially during the autumn, with harvesting achieved pratically overnight. A memory of our very first night spent on Whiteway soil is of the hum of a distant combine harvester working away in the darkness while we lay in bed listening. A few weeks later, I was treated to another farming ritual, that of burning the stubble. In the darkness the expanse of roaring flames was reflected in the pond, so creating a double effect, a visual pleasure never forgotten, and not repeated for many a long year.

Also, to the relief of many, now only a memory are the rats and mice. We managed to put up with the mice, who ate their way through all our packet foods, bought in bulk from the wholesalers, in preparation for the terrible winters which everyone had told us lay ahead. Our tinned foods were defiantly messed on in revenge for the unavailability of their contents, but when an odour developed which would not leave us, we smelled a rat, and that worried us.

*Those who have done all the work on their homes will know only too well the satisfaction gained, and the relief on completion. Sacrifices are made throughout though. If the weather is fine you should be working on it! What then about the children? You should be taking them out! Fear of a bad winter is usually a deciding factor. For us, the year without a roof and heating was the worst! The house, originally built in 1939 is on part of Sinclair's farmland.*
*(Photograph by Katrina Thacker)*

A few months later the odour disappeared. It was not until over a year later, when pulling up our bedroom floor to install further central heating pipes that we discovered its skeleton lying in its nest by the warm pipes, surrounded by its accumulated possessions. It had chosen my side of the bed, what a thought!

Rats were a common problem on Whiteway, probably because so many colonists kept chickens. It must have been a record year for them in 1934, for a Rat Week commencing on 11 June, was organised with George Barker being in charge of the poison and its preparation, and four other colonists to help him.

We do not have rats now, and since rebuilding our home, we have no mice either. Instead there are Mallards and their young, persistently building their nests, and laying their eggs each season. When successful, mother and chicks make their way almost immediately down to the lake, hopefully to grow and develop.

Whiteway has grown and developed, even since our arrival here, but not artificially. It has evolved as it always has done individually, and in keeping with its environment and nature.

# *Chapter 21*

# THE INTRODUCTION OF WATER AND ELECTRICITY SUPPLIES

In August 1949, Whiteway Colony gained its water supply. This followed ten months of trench digging, pipe installing and general upheaval. The supply travelled from Chalford, and forty-four colonists took advantage of its convenience.

The price of connection varied enormously, from £3 8s 11d for Trecarne, which sat very near the road and so took only a foot or so of pipe, to £36 4s 4d for Sunnymedes, way off the beaten track with many yards of excavation and pipework involved. The cost of connecting the Hall itself cost £46 16s 4d. The total for everyone came to £706 0s 6d. A mighty amount for such a small community just after the War. So, as it would have been unfair, not to say impossible, for those who lived furthest from the road to pay so much, it was decided that those who wished to be involved, should all pay an equal share, thus reducing each families' cost to the more reasonable sum of £16 16s 0d a house.

Some colonists refused to have the supply installed, only changing their minds at the last moment but insisting that it stayed outside where it belonged, in the form of a standpipe. Miss Kathleen Lee at the Nook was one such person, whereas Bea Adams at The Bungalow refused connection altogether, remaining content with her filtration system and pump in the kitchen.

It was not until 1989 that the water supply was eventually put into The Bungalow, when Mick and Doris paid £538.50, just so that they could flush their toilet.

The Dry Ground was the first piece of land to be affected, and many men worked long hours digging out the trenches initially with a digger, and then by hand with picks and shovels. Many a Sunday dinner was provided for them by colonists. The pipes were laid right up to the houses, but the trenches were not filled in, this part being left to the owner of the house to complete.

The Dry Ground road on which many hours of labour had been expended since its commencement in the twenties, was damaged in four places as a result of the upheaval. However, the small compensation offered by the Water Board was eventually accepted and contributed towards the purchase of materials which were used when a communal road repair effort was undertaken later on Sunday mornings.

So pleased were the people of Whiteway when the water was actually here and flowing freely to their homes that in August, a special social was held in the Hall, to which all the contractors and workers were invited. Harry Platt was in charge of the work. He was short and round, and always wore a dicky bow tie, even at work on the roads. This daytime adornment lit up by some means or another, whereas the one worn during the evening whizzed round like a propeller. While at Whiteway he lodged with Les and Mary Workman at Maurica.

Daily life now underwent a change. Prior to this time everyone had needed to fetch a supply of water each day. Most households had to come to the stream on the Wet Ground, where there was an overflow pipe from the Hazel Manor supply. This distance for those living at the far end of the Dry Ground was quite a step, especially if more than one journey was required. They could then choose if they wished to walk down over the back of Whiteway into Miserden Estate instead, the journey was a little shorter, but considerably steeper.

Whatever the arrangement regarding the daily supply, a large chunk in time must have been taken from each day, particularly if the family was large. A number of families though made their way to the Wet Ground stream, the

*Peter Parsons, a former engine driver, fetched his water this way, and you could set your watch by him! During winter months corrugated cardboard covered his legs. He lived on the Dry Ground in a round, corrugated iron hut, which was painted at first in a variety of colours like a rainbow, but eventually ended up black. He called it 'Opotiki' after a village in New Zealand where he had once lived. He had tremendous admiration for William Morris, and had a passion for collecting books. So much so that there was little space left in his hut in which he could live. The children would visit him there and he would tell them stories about trains. On his wall there were two pictures, both of the Tay Bridge, one when it was complete, and the other when it had collapsed.*

*Jeanne collecting her daily supply of water.*

*The Maxfield family who came in 1921 from Burnley, Lancashire. Alan and Elsie with toddler Enid. Tommy stands behind.*

Maxfields being one of them. Elsie and Alan used buckets but Enid, as a small child, had her own special container. Hers was an olive oil tin from the bakehouse. Others used yolks and some used jugs. The shortest route was always taken, resulting in a network of paths throughout the village, trodden down over the years, through gardens and along boundaries. Many of these have now fallen into disuse, and some Colonists whose land they crossed, are pleased that they are no longer needed.

The washing water was collected from the roofs in large water butts, and either used directly from there or, alternatively, it flowed into a filtration system which was dug out and constructed alongside the house. This water was also suitable for drinking after it had been processed through the charcoal. It was pumped up into a tank and drawn off from a tap usually situated in the kitchen.

There was another type of water filtration device also in use. This was a stoneware container, divided into two sections. About a gallon of rainwater was poured into the top half, which trickled very slowly through a charcoal layer into the lower part, straining out the tiddlers and bits of dirt. As this took some time, the container was usually filled up last thing at night, so that when morning a whole gallon of clear, drinking water was ready to be drawn off via the little tap at the bottom. The beauty of this was that it could stand indoors, and there was no leg work involved. Some colonists simply boiled their rainwater if it was clean and drank it as it was.

Before the water supply was installed washing was done in a variety of ways. Some people soaked it in their galvanised bath tubs overnight to loosen the dirt. The following day, after a good scrub on the scrubbing board with a chunk of Sunlight soap cut off the main block, it was either wrung out by hand, a task which required strong wrists, or put through the mangle, before being hung out to dry.

Others used a Dolly Tub, or even had a copper. For many years Leonie Blackwood soaked her washing in the bath, before having a brick copper installed in her newly-built bathroom. It had a copper inset, and was designed to heat water for both bathing and washing. She recalls how this proved such a fiddle with its lighting and filling, that it was easier to carry the water from the range, which was what she usually ended up doing. Another method involved using the primus stove with a bucket on the top.

The first washing machine used by Joy Evans was a round wooden tub, with a fly wheel on the lid, and a wooden device resembling a stool inside. This was filled with hot water, and the handle on the top used to activate the washing inside. A wringer was attached to finish the job off. Later Joy became the owner of a galvanised square washing machine, which also had a wringer and single blade for activating. Underneath, a large primus stove heated the water to the required temperature so allowing it to boil on the spot. Both of these were used after the connection of mains water, but still had to be filled by bucket as the weekly wash was done in the shed in the garden.

There was also another type very similar to the one used by Joy. This too was square, with paddles inside rotated by a handle, but there was no heating device with this model and no wringer.

The ironing that followed was done with flat irons, one in use while the other was warming up. Both Leonie and Elsie Maxfield heated their irons on a primus, especially in the summertime when the range was unlit.

They, like most of the rest of the colonists owned a black-leaded range, with the oven at the back and the fire towards the front. Elsie kept a large container to heat the water throughout the day on the top of hers, so that hot water was constantly available for that bath in front of the fire or for any other purpose. Leonie's was slightly different, having a tank with the capacity of about two gallons incorporated into the side. This meant that she too always had hot water on tap if she remembered to top it up each time she drew some off. Both were fuelled with coal, but Leonie and many more, I expect, went wooding in Miserden woods to supplement the supply.

It is interesting to see which electrical appliance was most popular when electricity was first installed. Leonie's was a dry iron. She hated the fiddle of the old method and remembers the bliss and ease of using the modern type. There was a pressure iron available then which was filled with paraffin and primed up, so dispensing with all the to-ing and fro-ing associated with the use of a flat iron but the majority usually prefered the tried and tested way. After the iron, Leoni invested in a small washing machine, followed later by a cooker.

Some homes had bathrooms before the mains water supply was connected, The Bungalow and Bidwell being two such examples. The Maxfields, like most other families on Whiteway, did not have their bathroom until mains water was available and the Mardells did not have one at all until 1966. Judy was married before the Mardells were able to bathe in their modern blue bathroom, just off the kitchen. Until then they had continued with the tin bath in front of the kitchen fire, filling it with hot water from the fire which had a back boiler.

Now that water was freely available, it became possible for flush toilets to be installed. Previously the Elsan or Wet and Dry bucket toilets were commonly used. With the latter, which some preferred as no chemicals were required and their contents could be safely used on the garden, two holes were sited side by side, sometimes a lean-to next to the coal and wood store, thus avoiding the need to venture outside.

The use of flush toilets could only be achieved with the addition of a septic tank, as no mains sewerage was available at Whiteway then or indeed today. The option to be connected was offered in 1974, but as the septic tanks had proved adequate, and the cost and upheaval would have been phenomenal, the majority decided against the plan.

The drainage at our end of the Wet Ground is exceptionally good due, I am informed, to the quantity of rock. We had personal proof of this when, with the assistance of a pneumatic drill and two strong friends, we excavated a huge pile, which took three years to clear away.

The septic tanks have to take a good deal more now than when initially installed. The twin tub washing machine that most used in the 1960's and '70's has now made way for the automatic, although some homes still have a soak-away for some of their water outlets as we do.

Another commodity which required regular collection was paraffin. This was used widely in Whiteway homes for heating, lighting and cooking. On reflection it was dangerous but vital, with it being required to fuel so many appliances.

The Wexhams sold paraffin at their small shop at Sainfoin during some of the earlier years, as did Bea Adams at The Bungalow. She had a supply tank in her shed and colonists could go there to buy small amounts from her. She also sold other basic necessities, which came by train from Mapletons, the vegetarian wholesalers at Liverpool, and had to be collected from the station by horse and cart. Vivian Lewis' garage and the Bakehouse were also suppliers of paraffin. If larger quantities of paraffin were required and storage was available, then it was possible to do as the Maxfields and purchase five gallons or so at a time from Bert Canton at Sheepscombe, storing it in their own tank in the cellar.

Most people will probably remember how dirty it made the house and certainly the resulting smell. Regular cleaning of appliances was necessary to prevent them from smoking. I can remember how, even into the seventies, paraffin was still used for oilstove heaters, even though electricity was available then.

Electricity came to Whiteway five years after the water supply, the Dry Ground being first to be connected. They were 'switched on' by Christmas Eve 1954. The Light Family at The Long Hut were, appropriately, one of the first ones to be 'lit up'. Pearl recalls that the MEB wired them up, and how when she went out it was not there and when she returned it was!

Her first buy was a Baby Belling cooker, closely followed by an iron. The Maxfield household was also ready for Christmas, expertly wired up by Alan whose profession it was, and so knew of such things. Their first purchase was a spanking new Belling Cooker, which stood proudly next to the faithful old paraffin one, waiting to cast its spell over the most important meal of the year, Christmas dinner. But when the time came to try it out, Elsie's confidence flew out the window, and she reverted instead to her old tried and trusted oil cooker, so leaving her new acquisition clean and sparkling for yet another day.

Those on the Wet Ground had to wait a bit longer for their supply. Not too long though, for by 17 February 1955, everyone had been wired up, the final house to be connected was The Cabin, belonging to Douglas White.

Most people were pleased with the cleanness and brightness, although one said that they preferred the soft glow of their oil lamps. Several others remembered how they missed the warmth given off by the lamps, for two were usually needed to provide adequate light in a good sized sitting room! The Maxfields had one which hooked onto the wall in their sitting room and Judy can remember doing her homework by an Aladdin lamp in the Workshop's kitchen, and cooking toast and sausages over an oilstove.

Primus cooking in several forms was common to all. There was a Beatrice stove which having a straight wick needed no priming and was ideal for slow cooking, but smoked if it was turned up too high. The Florence which was much bigger stood on the floor, and had two or three burners. It was as tall as a full-sized cooker and constructed from angle iron, with a heavily enamelled metal top. The burners were of varying sizes with the one at the oven end biggest of all. The oven itself was large, stretching from the front to the back. There was a glass tank which held a gallon of paraffin, fitted with a needle through which it was automatically fed. Joy had a Florence stove in her kitchen at The Makins, preferring its versatility, so much so that she kept it until 1958, only changing it when her daughter Rosalind began secondary school and cookery classes.

Archie Turner, another resident who owned a shop in Gloucester selling bottled gas, supplied some colonists with Bottogas, around the time of Second World War. He had lived in America and still spoke with an American accent. He was also a business man, capable of making a large amount of money one minute, and equally capable of spending it all the next.

He came up with the idea that bottled gas was a commodity necessary in rural areas. In December 1940 at 5.30 am, some of his bottles exploded at his home, causing everyone to think that an air-raid was taking place. Fortunately his house was saved from burning down, but perhaps his business suffered a bit through lack of confidence although Mary Robert was brave enough to have this method of cooking installed at Wayside.

Mick and Doris had come from London and were already accustomed to modern living, but reverted to the old ways for their Whiteway life. Now they had to change again, discovering to their horror that their television set had developed green spot while in storage. Mick was lucky though on another count, for the people who installed his electricity, also erected a television aerial for him.

The radio was a firm favourite with many, allowing the world and its news into the home, without anyone having to step outside the door. Leonie says that this was the beginning of the gradual decrease in social life. Even before the advent of electricity, battery operated radios were commonly available. A man would come regularly to collect the batteries, which would be taken away and re-charged, ready for exchange on his next delivery, many people took advantage of this service.

Then came television, which persuaded even more people to stay at home for entertainment. Characters from radio and television became 'friends' to stay in for, and could be enjoyed without taking the trouble to go out into the cold. Some say that 'the electric' changed Whiteway, and it was never the same again.

There were more tradesmen delivering to Whiteway during those early years. The first postal delivery to Whiteway which anyone can remember was by bicycle from Slad Post Office. When larger items such as parcels had to come up around Christmas time, they were brought by pony and cart.

Leonie remembers that the postman did not wear a uniform. In fact, it seems only a comparatively recent occurrence for postmen here on Whiteway to dress in official garb. Mr Woolf, when he ran the Post Office at Camp, and delivered the mail never wore anything resembling what most people regard as proper uniform. I am told that he began by riding a bicycle to make his deliveries, but I can only remember him with his motorbike, the engine of which gradually increased in volume as he rode nearer and nearer to Whiteway across the fields from Camp in the early morning. I well remember the first time I saw him, and the surprise I felt, for here was someone more resembling Sherlock Holmes with his clipped in trousers and deer stalker hat, than the postmen I was used to.

In about 1930, Harry Palmer can recall Howard Nation who lived at Bisley delivering the mail on his push bike and Jo Mardell remembers doing the Christmas post as a student in 1949 with a lady postwoman called Joyce. Joyce delivered to the villages, while Jo cycled to the outlying farms. There was a delivery on Christmas Day in those days.

Milk deliveries by Sidney Hall began after he had bought Bidwell Farm from Rachelle. Until then all milk was collected, but Sidney walked round the Colony, filling up the jugs that were left by the doors. The round was confined to Whiteway, for Miserden had its own milk supply from Henley Farm. When Bidwell Farm was sold, towards the end of the thirties, George

Parker who eventually bought the Kenworthy's Carriers stables took over this essential service. The round gradually increased in size over the years until, when the Goulbournes began living there, it included Miserden as well. Joy can never remember having cream from them though. She was usually sent over to the Dickinsons farm at Bidfield for any luxuries such as this.

Another basic essential that was delivered to Whiteway, despite there not really being a need for it there, was bread from the Painswick Bakery. Only those living near the public road could buy this, for that was as far as the van ventured. Everyone knew that Protheroe's bread was best, and sought after by the whole of the country, but even so occasionally some rebels deserted it for a sliced loaf.

As Ethel Portlock lived nearer to the road than anyone, and was in the habit of availing herself of their services, anyone who wished to get a Painswick loaf could ask her to get extra, and their problem was solved. Similarly the Co-operative Grocery mobile services visited Whiteway, and as they offered a different selection of foods they found that coming here was worth their while.

The Bakery used solid fuel for many a year until it converted to oil. My father supplied it, together with other houses, at one stage. Years ago, when my grandfather made deliveries up here with his horse and cart it was a day's trip. His two-wheeled cart would come laden, with all his customers buying in large quantities, filling their cellars ready for the winter. Today a lorry comes round with a sack or two, every week, delivering in one day to all those who require it.

Colonists have said how there was always someone on the road, fetching something. It was impossible to go out without meeting someone on their way for water, milk, fuel, to shop or just visiting. People visited a lot more then. Today the lanes are quiet. You may see someone walking, but it is more likely that they will be in a car, waving and mouthing to you as they rush by.

Before this modern means of transport, which is so essential today as the buses are so few, public transport played a major part in the colonists lives, being their main outlet for work, shopping or pleasure. As in most villages, the need for people to leave their community was probably more on a weekly or even monthly basis than daily as now and transport was provided by Wests of Sheepscombe. With the advent of the motor car Carters of Miserden was available, as in later years was Vivian Lewis at The Tea Pot, especially for night trips when the bus service had ended for the day.

It was on 18 April 1927 when the Red Bus Company began a service from Stroud to Cheltenham via Wateredge. This was so successful that only three weeks later it extended its route to include Sheepscombe, Wishanger,

*The Red and White Bus.*

Miserden and Whiteway. This meant that a whole new world was opened up to these rural communities.

That same July, seeing possibilities in store for them also, another bus company, The National, came upon the transport scene with their route from Stroud to Birdlip, so ensuring for those at Whiteway and the other villages on the route, six buses each day, a spoiling of choice to all. During the fifties there was still a very regular service, and the buses were always full, so much so that in 1941 Western National was requested to consider that those who resided in outlying districts were provided for, and those who lived nearer the town did not take up all the seats. There is little danger of this happening today, for even the two or sometimes three visits daily which we now have, only attracts the school child, and maybe one or two others sitting solitarily on the bus with most of the seats at their disposal.

# *Chapter 22*
# A Childhood View of Whiteway in the 1970's and 1980's

By now I expect you have gathered a wealth of impressions of how Whiteway started and developed from the early settlers to the newcomers to the present inhabitants of the Colony. I would like to add to these by describing Whiteway from my point of view – Vicky Thacker, having grown up on Whiteway during the seventies and eighties and not necessarily being aware of the principles on which Whiteway is based.

With most people being unfamiliar with Whiteway's history, I was most amused when friends in my secondary school, Stroud Girls' High School, on hearing where I lived commented on how it used to be a nudist colony. Naturally, I just smiled and assured them it was not today (or at least not as far as I had seen!). A certain amount of mystery was also added by us Whiteway children only having a small mini-bus to travel home on whilst all the other children in Stroud's surrounding area had double-decker buses.

We were also the ones who were always late when it snowed, as it always seems to drift up around Whiteway when a few flakes have been scattered on Stroud. You can imagine how, as children, we used to listen intently to the travel news, hoping that the Whiteway bus would be cancelled. It inevitably was! Unfortunately the mums would always group together, risking accidents on those icy roads, to bring us down in car loads. Another impression of Whiteway I gained from my friends was that as they drove through the colony trying to find my house they were amazed how many houses there were behind the facade of the few houses and much foliage which fronted the main road. A friend from polytechnic always refers to the 'mud huts' that we live in when I describe what Whiteway is like and how we sound like hippies living in a commune with our collectively held land. When you think about it, it is no wonder that over the years some people have acquired such a distorted perception of Whiteway.

As a child, I have the happy recollection of feeling completely free to play behind Whiteway in the woods, which belong to Miserden Estate, to play in the stream on the Wet Ground or climb trees and make tree houses all day long until it was time for tea. Whiteway has always been a comfortable place for children to grow up in as everyone uses first names. A long tradition which developed from the idea of complete equality amongst the colonists.

*In the garden of The Retreat in 1974. Kirsten Budgeon (Joy and Peter's grand-daughter) with Katrina and Victoria Thacker.*

This meant that as a child you were not cut off from the adults by formality. This was emphasised for me by going to Hilda Gustin's house, where she always made us very welcome by giving us Ribena to drink and letting us play in her naturally wild and overgrown garden. She had a stream running through the bottom of her garden so we would build dams in it and play on the trees which had fallen over it. We are also lucky to have a neighbour, Elsie Johnson, who let us have fires and build walls on her land. Looking back on this, children on Whiteway seem to feel instinctively that the land is everybody's as there is never the air of restriction when 'hanging about' on the Sports Field or stirring up the embers of the fire in front of the Hall after Bonfire Night.

There are specific social events, which have continued from the time of the early pioneers, such as gathering together on special occasions. I remember as a very small child going to the bonfire night celebration, which were organised by the Play Group on the corner of the sport's field. Then there was the Children's Christmas party in the Hall with a large spread of goodies laid out and later in the evening a meeting with Santa. Everyone was welcome, making it seem like a huge family party as both adults and children joined in the games together.

As previously mentioned another favourite night was Bonfire Night. Everyone walked down to the hall in their warmest clothes, admired the Guy usually artistically made by Mike Hawkes, ate all the hot-dogs they could and marvelled at the fireworks. As a child, I remember watching a firework which released a parachute, seeing where it fell. Everyone would be out around the hall and in the cow's field next day looking for it, as it was considered quite a prize. It is nice to think that these events continue today, as they did all those years ago, with those who were children then bringing their own children and even grandchildren along to join in the festivities.

I can also remember going carol singing around the Colony a few weeks before Christmas. Anyone could join in as long as they could see one of the computer printed carol sheets which were used every year. People of all ages and vocal abilities joined us and when we had sung a particularly good rendition of a favourite carol then one of the elderly people we used to visit would distribute sweets and other goodies to us children. The Playgroup mothers still carry on this tradition though with fewer people than before but it is still a nice surprise to open the door to such cheerful singers.

Thinking about going from door to door brings back memories of Halloween night, when it was quite safe for us to go round as we knew everyone on the Colony so had none of the fears that modern-day children have. The only worry that we would have was of someone jumping out at us from behind a bush or just bumping into us in the darkness of the lanes. Even the branch of a tree can be frightening when there are no street lights to see by.

A privilege unique to Whiteway and its children is the Whiteway swimming pool. This would be the envy of all the other children on a hot day during the summer. I am sure that many a child has learnt to swim there, and although chlorine is used, it is only in mild doses and therefore much less irritating to a child's eyes than the water in a council pool. The pool becomes the social meeting place during the Summer as the Sheep Dip was for the pioneers. Many a time I can remember begging my mum to let me remain in the care of my friends' mums so I could stay an extra hour. Childhood is a time when it is useful to have all the colonists together, being able to trust their children to the care of others.

Around Christmas time, the snow would come and everyone would look forward to sledging and sacking in Mr Goulbourne's field. All the colony children would come together to see who could go fastest down the hill, hopefully missing the frozen cow-pats. If you had a particulary good sledge like the Branhams or overloaded it, there was always the danger of smashing through the wooden fence at the bottom and ending up on the Parish road. I can remember on one occasion, all of us children sitting at the top of the field, chatting together at 11 o'clock, waiting to go night-sledging. Looking back, in this day and age when children want more sophisticated amusements, inevitably in towns, Whiteway seems unique in providing a secure atmosphere where parents could let their children go off and play, so long as it was within the security of Colony land.

Other memories include going up to the Goulbourne's farm to collect bottles of unpasteurised milk when we ran out. It is funny that this seemed as natural then as buying milk from a shop does now. The farm was very much a part of Whiteway, even though it is on non-Colony land. As a child one does not make the distinction between who lives on Colony land and who does not. The feeling is one of a village together.

I also recall going down to the shop at the bakery to buy penny sweets, invariably seeing other colonists arriving around the corner when I left, although, strangely, the shop came over as being very private and usually empty. This is because it was originally set up with the idea that the colonists be self-sufficient within the community. It was not set on the main road as other village shops were so did not attract passing trade. Unfortunately the shop and the bakery business are now no more so it is necessary to venture out of the Colony to pick up essential items.

These fond childhood memories are, I suspect, also prominent for others of my era, and I would say that as a child, Whiteway seemed to me like any other village, although lacking certain amenities within its centre such as more than two to three buses a day and a pub or a church. Despite this, I think Whiteway Colony is a wonderful place in which to bring up children (as is demonstrated by those returning in abundance with their own families), as it retains a certain innocence that only an isolated place can.

Being involved with this book and learning more about Whiteway's history, makes me feel proud to have been a part of it. I do not think that children fully realise the significance behind owning or not owning the land and it seems a shame that when they do get to learn about the land-holding system, they do not understand the principles and reasons behind it. I hope this book will give them a better idea of their heritage and that they will come to regard Whiteway as more than just an isolated village with no fun, as is the view often held during teenage years.

# *Chapter 23*
# THE NON-WHITEWAY LAND

There have been occasions throughout this book when the 'non-Whiteway' land has been mentioned, and an explanation may be useful to show its relationship with the Colony. The land forms part of the village, but is not the Colony, as the land is held privately and not communally. None of its ten houses were there at the Colony's formation, the first one probably being built about 1909.

For many years only two houses existed, each occupying approximately equal amounts of land. However during the twenties, and then the sixties, the land was sold off, other dwellings built, and the number there today was reached. Four of these are newer replacements for less substantial predecessors, all of which were built along similar lines to those on Colony land.

The land was acquired by the first owners in the following way. During the spring of the Colony's first year, 1899, a letter was received from a Farmer Causey in Wiltshire, who had had to sell his land when a compulsory purchase order was placed on it by the Government, who required it for their own activities. Disheartened and discouraged with the system because of this action, and having heard of Whiteway where the sympathetic approach to life was so similar to that which now engulfed him, he decided to investigate. This was with an eye to purchasing the adjoining eighty acres of land that were still available with his government pay-off money, and integrating with Whiteway in some form, on a communally beneficial basis.

The colonists accepted his application, although Eiloart had some reservations about admitting a person with so much personal wealth. He arrived with a flock of sheep and two men who, by getting drunk the first weekend, did little to improve the colony's poor reputation. A little later, his sister came with the cows, which were put to graze on the Dry Ground field. Farmer Causey and his men were able to live in some collapsible huts which they had brought along with them and his sister stayed with Jeannie in Whiteway House.

All worked out excellently for a few months, with each party sharing their produce with the other.

The crop of sainfoin which occupied the Colony land when purchased, was cut by the farmer's machinery in gratitude for his use of the Dry

Ground field. With everyone working together happily during that first summer, there were expectations of a productive future ahead.

Having thought the situation through, the farmer bought the other eighty acres of land across the stream, but before anything further could be done, the Bracher *vs* Colony confrontation occurred, with its aspects of instability. This resulted in the Causeys removing themselves over onto their land immediately, taking with them about eight potential colonists from Bristol. There they proclaimed they would run their own organisation on more methodical lines!

*The Stroud Weekly Press* reports on 8 September 1899,

> Mr Causey, a farmer tired of agriculture as a source of profit, relinquished his tenancy of nearly 1000 acres of land at the other end of the country, and threw in his lot with the Whiteway Communists. A few weeks elapsed, and finding that he could not work with them, purchased 80 acres of land adjoining, and about a dozen intended joining him in cultivation of it. At first, it will now be a Colony and at any time only those who accept Christ as the Head and Guide of all will be admitted into the circle. They each believe they have a part to play in life, and having played that part, they will be open to receive others, and give them the benefit of their labours.

It continued, 'Idlers will not be tolerated by the new group. 'Moral invaders' will be told that unless they work, they will not eat'.

The article continues to explain that although as yet they had no houses, because of their inventiveness they had turned their twenty-foot cowshed into a fine dining-room, and were well on the way to constructing a large wooden dormitory. It further elaborates on the fact that equipped with twenty cows, six or seven horses, and a flock of poultry, together with Miss Causey's expertise as a dairy woman, 'Everything at present appears to augur for success.'

This optimistic forecast proved unfounded, for although productive initially, with the provision of a house and outbuildings, the scheme eventually failed. In around 1915 the land was sold, interestingly enough into the estate from where it originally came, now in the possession of Colonel Bonham.

In about 1909, a portion of Causeys farmland adjoining the council road and known as Clay Piece was sold into private ownership. Will Cole one of its new owners was in occupation at this time. Also George and Fred Kenworthy with their sister Agnes were at Highfields just across the road. They were John Colman Kenworthy's children.

When Farmer Causey embarked on the sale of his land, the Kenworthys also purchased a piece of land parallel with Dairy Lane leading to Sinclair's farm. From the stables erected there, they ran their carrier's business, selling up in 1930 to Miss Hendrika Eilers, sister to Fritz a Dutchman, who converted the cart sheds into a dwelling while renting Highfields from the Kenworthys. He used the surrounding buildings and land for his poultry business, and christened the whole enterprise Hilltop Farm.

During the short while the farm was in their possession Fritz married Margaret or 'Peggie'. I have conformation of this happy occasion in the form of a small printed card which they sent out to neigbours and friends. Two words at the bottom perhaps sum up their financial situation during those difficult times. They are 'No Reception'. A bit sad!

Financially, circumstances must have improved for them, for within three years Fritz had bought The Red House, and because his sister had sold the farm, his poultry business was moved over there, where he not only used the land surrounding his house, but the future Sports Field ground as well for his ever increasing chicken runs.

When one of his chick houses was destroyed by fire, Fritz was badly burned trying to put it out. Shortly afterwards he gave up the business, sold the Red House, and moved to the Wet Ground part of the colony taking one of his remaining chicken houses with him to convert into a home, for he and Peggie to live in.

Hilltop Farm was bought by Allen, Jones and Gardner, Mrs Dekkers, Mr Hacklin and the Parkers during the 1930s. It is now in the Goulbourne family.

Dennis Boynton, mentioned many times, built and lived at Stonecott. He was friendly with Arkle the builder, who lived in his own house at Miserden, now owned by the Estate. Encouraged by him, he began to dig out stone to form a cellar, from which he constructed the house. He was very young at the time being only eighteen years old.

The house was to be for his parents who, with their family, had previously lived at the Studio on Whiteway land. When the building was only half finished Dennis ran out of money, and emigrated to America to earn more working as a lumberjack. On his return, he completed his building, and he and his parents moved in. The year '1924' is carved on the house, but whether this is the completion date is not known, for Leonie Blackwood recollects going there as a child, and she was born in 1906, so it may be there for an another reason.

After Dennis' marriage to Annie, George Allen's daughter, they lived with George at Woodview, until his parents moved back to Leicestershire to live, and then he and Annie moved to Stonecott and made it their home. While there he kept pigs, and the relics of his piggery are towards the rear of Stonecott's garden. He also dug a well, which is in what is now the corner of Glendalough's property, Dennis' land, which originally stretched down to Dairy Lane having been divided into several parts, and built upon.

The well is between 35 and 45 feet deep, and the pump, serving it, was bought in America while he was working there. In the early days when water had to be fetched, Dennis' family was spared the ordeal of having to collect their daily supply from the watering hole, for on Stonecott's deeds it states that they were legally able to use the very source of the Holy Brook stream situated in Causeys own farmyard.

Leonie and her step brother, Bill Allen, sometimes stayed for the day with Annie at Stonecott, when her mother was busy. Annie sometimes bought bread from the Painswick Bakery, and a slice of this, spread with golden syrup was a treat which they always looked forward to, with no feeling of guilt whatsoever, despite the fact that it came from the 'opposition'. Jeannie Protheroe did not worry either when, in order to avail herself of the butter and cream which she favoured, she obtained both from the Causey's farm, and not from Sinclair's.

Oswald Allen was the next owner and he sold the house to Bernard Gabbott in 1939, who lived there with his wife Mabel, known as Billy, and children. An agreement was reached between them whereby he could live in Dennis' former workshop, just a few yards from the house. One day he went off and never returned. Bernard was a conscientious objector during the 1914–18 War and was always sympathetic to those of such views who came during the years of the Second World War. Peter, his son lives there today.

Lambert Smith bought the adjacent piece of land in 1923, on which he built himself a wooden house called Greenholme. Lambert who had been born in nearby Wishanger, learned to drive a huge old Wolseley car, belonging to Captain Brennon, at the tender age of thirteen whilst a garden boy at Miserden House. He was so small that he had to sit on a cushion in order to reach the pedals.

On his discharge from the Army in 1919, he returned to the Whiteway area and began employment with Protheroe's Bakery, where he worked for so many years. He was proud of his house, particularly the filtration water system which he installed there. In 1928 on the break up of his marriage, he moved out, his wife Lilian and their baby Brian continued to live there on their own. Lilian died in 1969 and their wooden house has since been demolished and replaced by a modern bungalow.

The land next to Lambert's was occupied by Will Cole, a market gardener who was a conscientious objector. His land also included that on which now stands yet another new bungalow. He was married to Dinah Partridge.

Clover Cottage is tucked away in the furthest corner of the land sold off by Causey.

The land was bought by Jeanne Marin, and her son Gustave partially built the house upon it. The original plot extended down to the road, but a pre-fab was erected on this lower part, which was eventually pulled down, to make way for the new bungalow which is there today.

The early occupiers of this land, although not officially Whiteway Colonists had many involvements with Colony affairs. Their attitudes were practically identical, and they more or less regarded themselves as colonists. The early Colony meetings were attended by them, and their ideas, with any offered advice were considered.

When a new formal system of meeting procedure was introduced in 1910, with a chairman and voting, those non-Whiteway land members were unable to cast a vote. In June 1912, a letter signed by those involved was read at the meeting, indicating that recently they were made to feel unwelcome in Colony affairs. They stated that they would like to know where they stood.

Arthur Ryland who lived in a bungalow in the mushroom field along the Calf Way writes,

> You will doubtless remember that three months ago, having taken up a very unpopular line with regard to George Allen's tithe, I was informed from the chair that not being a Whiteway colonist I had no business to interfere. Having waited to see whether the minute of the above mentioned meeting at which I was elected would be referred to, and finding that it was not done I had no other course than to conclude . . . that having acted contrary to the opinion of the majority, I was to consider myself as turned out of the colony, or at any rate put into my right place outside. . . .

He continues,

> I am still occasionally treated as a colonist myself by some members. I feel I should like the matter to be settled one way or another. Personally I stand exactly where I stood all along, I am willing to regard myself and the land I occupy as part and parcel of Whiteway Colony, if I am to be admitted, not on sufferance, but as a full member of the Colony.

He concludes,

> I am quite willing to join hands with the Colony on the same footing as before, and to enter loyally into the life of the community. If however this is not done, I have no other course open than to remain aloof.

The content of his letter was discussed and finally a conclusion was reached. A definition stated simply that, 'A Whiteway Colonist is a person who holds land on Whiteway.' Also added was the fact that honourary members could attend meetings if elected by three-quarters of the meeting's members, but Colonists only were eligible to vote.

Arthur and George Kenworthy were there and elected honourary members by all present, the minutes of the meeting were then sent in a letter to those concerned expressing the wish that they would again be involved with Whiteways activities.

The letter received was tongue in cheek, but struck the very heart of the matter.

> We the undersigned, ex Whiteway Colonists and members of the House of Lords, desire Humbly to thank the faithful Commons for so generously relieving us of the onerous duties of government, by de-franchising us and depriving us of membership of the aforesaid Whiteway Colony which we have hitherto held.

They also hoped that those two other non-Whitewayans, Will Cole and Fred Kenworthy, not blessed with Honourary status as yet, would soon also receive such privileges.

From that time, only the Kenworthys attended colony meetings, and then only when business matters required it. The voting policies adopted then only lasted for three years, being discontinued in favour of the old informal method. A decision to discontinue the attendance of visitors was also made, and this has remained in force from that time forth.

The people who live on the non-Whiteway land are still included in Whiteway social events and have never been excluded from the Children's Christmas Party, Bonfire night or Playgroup activities. This will continue.

# *Chapter 24*

# Whiteway Now Compared to Then

So how then has Whiteway Colony changed since our forefathers chose to abandon the restraints of Victorian values, for liberty, with all the ensuing problems?

Many things seem to have come full circle. The rates, despised by those early socialists, so much so that imprisonment was more acceptable to them than demeaning themselves to its payment, has during the past few years, disguised itself under a new name, that of the Poll Tax. As with our Whiteway pioneers, some are willing to suffer gaol rather than pay for something they feel is unfair.

The reasons are various. In Whiteway's case a reluctance to succumb to payment of a tax on property which they claimed they did not own and so had no legal right over, and with the Poll tax, the injustice of those with little contributing the same as those with much. Now all are united in their views.

Francis Sedlak wrote in *The New Order* in 1901,

> We do not trouble the Government. Nor are we much annoyed by its attempts to interfere with our peaceful life. In fact but for the Tax collector we should nearly forget that there exists any Government at all. Never the less so little heed is being paid to his notices that I have not yet been able to ascertain the exact amount of taxes. I suppose they are between seven and eight pounds. However who has to pay them? . . . the poor tax-collector hardly knows to whom to address his notices. He tries as were his luck, now with this one, now with that, of the members and always with little chance. The time for payment expires and then a summons from the Court makes its due appearance. On one occasion a member was imprisoned for fourteen days. At the time of writing two summons are pending. . . . If a summons were addressed to me, I should appear before the Court in order to show my good-will.

Needless to say, at the onset of individual living, it became their own affair, and all here today react exactly as the rest of society.

Clothes have always been an outward sign of the feeling within oneself

*One of three Oxford undergraduates who cycled to Whiteway wearing this distinctive style of dress in 1921. They were Marcus Bantok, Michael Cardew the Art Potter, and Martin Harvey an actor. The freedom of movement it allowed made it instantly popular with some colonists, with a variety of fabrics used to suit mood and season, although it was discarded after several chilly years.*

and one's surrounding environment. Therefore from the outset, even though there was no written constitution, distinctive changes were visibly made by all. Former incumbrances of corsets and long skirts, stiff collars and boots were dispensed with so proclaiming to the world that a revolution was taking place. All the men grew their hair long, tying it back in a pigtail as often seen now.

We all recall modes of dress during our lives which speak volumes on national and social situations, without uttering a word. What about the fifties with the emergence of rock and roll, accompanied by the extrovert dress of the Teddy boys, or the sixties flaunting newly found sexual freedom with the mini skirt. This public announcement by way of attire, drew attention to the 'new people's' cause, telling the world of their opposition to the tight regimented structure of the day. It was always referred to in newspaper columns, along with the story of nudism and free love.

*Youngsters in the sheep dip. Bidwell is the house behind.*

In modern times perhaps only nudism would gain a second glance, clothes and free union, though not necessarily free love, being commonplace. The open discussion, so important then, allowed any guilt to be dispelled, as it does today. We then find in consequence, avenues hitherto closed, opened and explored, so leading to an expression of life not embarked upon before.

The nudism saga, no doubt brought about by the conspicuous lack of covering on the body so noticable at the turn of the century, and boosted by the sheep dip episodes, brought char-a-bancs of inquisitive sightseers along the public road running through the Colony's centre. Any conversation associated with Whiteway, always managed to include nudism, often when the subject was initially of an entirely different nature. Even today, I can almost guarantee that within a few moments of conversation with a person who has heard of Whiteway, but knows little about it, they will say, 'Isn't that where the nudists live?' or 'That used to be a nudist colony didn't it?'.

One or two real nudists have come, believing in what they had heard, and determined to try it out, but their behaviour has not been accepted generally, and I can safely say that to there is no nudism here now, although we all know how some swimming costumes leave little to the imagination. One schoolgirl in the 1940s was making the somewhat lengthy bus journey home from Stroud, with two ladies sitting behind her who conversed with each other at length on the subject of Whiteway Colony. The nudism story came up as always, and as the journey progressed, the schoolgirl got crosser and crosser. Eventually they arrived at the 'Whiteway Nudist Colony' where the bus stopped to let the girl off, at which she stood up, turned to the two women and said, 'Well I live here, do I look like a nudist?'

There have on occasions been enquiries to our Colony about nudism. One such came in July 1924. It was a circular regarding the formation of a Sun-Ray Club. As this arrived when Whiteway was enjoying its phase of dipping in the stream, following Stormont's lectures, then all agreed that a letter should be written asking for the ideas surrounding its formation and activities, and whether an affiliated group was available to join. There was a reply a few weeks later stating that through lack of response in the British Isles, the idea had been abandoned. So much for nudism, especially on these wind swept hills.

The subject of free love has recieved much attention. Free union is the correct phrase, and those who have undertaken it, are as serious as those who undertake any legal bonds. Marriage, or the lack of it, is acceptable now throughout the country. The horror and pity once extended to relatives on hearing of its avoidance, has now moderated. Couples pair up, buy houses and produce families, often without the pressure from their peers which existed not too long ago.

It is difficult then for us to understand the stigma which was placed on those who opposed the tradition of centuries, when a lengthy engagement 'to get to know each other' was followed by a proper white wedding, all done correctly and in public for all to witness, the purity of the bride, even into the sixties was still very important.

May's parents were probably appalled at their daughter's free union with Mac, and she must have had amazing courage to breakaway from her roots to achieve it. Even in later decades, girls who brought shame to their families were sent away to the country to have their babies secretly, the situation being best kept under wraps.

The free union tradition at Whiteway and other similar communities, had a shock effect, for it too is often mentioned early in a conversation. Those who wanted to seal their relationship in this way usually did so publicly. There would be an announcement to the other members of the Colony, which was received with as much pleasure as any traditional engagement.

One couple who felt the need to legalize their union in 1919 did so almost fervently, a matter which took a while for them to live down, for by then free union had become to them a normal occurrence, a 'marriage' by trust and love, not one often tied by the fetters of vows. Even so, there was nothing wrong in legal union, for many of the colony's early settlers were already married, and if those involved felt good about it, then that surely was all that mattered.

The woman often retained her own name, to prove that she was not shackled to a man simply because of their being together, either in marriage or free union. It is perhaps a little confusing to an outsider, as to who went with whom, because those on Whiteway normally used their first names.

Whiteway today seems to be perhaps 'above average' in its legally married population. I was told by Leonie when she was a young woman that no-one was married in church, if they wanted to legalize their union then it was off to the registry office, but then few went to Church anyway.

Some now, are church attenders though, or they hold meeting in a private house, as the Society of Friends does. In many villages the church is the hub of its life. Apart from its worshipping aspect, its tendrils reach out through social activities to all there, whether through the Mother's Union, visits in time of sickness, advice on family matters from the vicar or involvement with weddings or funerals. There is very little it does not touch, even schooling, as at Miserden, many days each term entail contact with the church in some form. It binds the whole together.

This applies also to the 'Lord of the Manor' system, common to most villages at the turn of the century. The role being one of traditional protection. The lord's patronage inevitably dominated the whole village, which sometimes was owned by him. One can then understand the release that Whiteway gave to those used to this claustrophobic atmosphere for each person here was his own master, reliant on no-one but himself.

The aforementioned christian name tradition is as common on Whiteway today, as it ever was. I can recall being asked by a delivery driver even after I had lived here some time, where a Mrs Blackwood lived at house called Panelis. I can remember telling him that no-one of that name lived on Whiteway, and there was not a house called that here either, and sent him along to Miserden. Now if he had said Leonie there would have been no trouble at all!

It took some getting used to, coming here from where 'Aunty' and 'Uncle' must, through courtesy, be affixed to the christian name of any one older than oneself. Now after being here for twenty-five years, I think that I have just about mastered it.

House names had been confusing too. Houses previously gained recognition through their appearance and surroundings which must have been difficult when there were five studios, two shacks and many bungalows. Once when there was a competition in the Hall, in which the object was fitting suitable names to each dwelling, Alan Maxfield's house gained the name of Symphony because it had remained 'unfinished' for so long. This name stuck, so at least dispensing with yet another bungalow.

Occupations on Whiteway are varied; there are here now businesses, some one-man concerns, others employing staff, crafts people, and many others working outside, but prosperous or not, everyone here is viewed from the same standpoint. Somehow on Whiteway one's way of earning a living does not hold the importance it might elsewhere. The pioneers would be pleased that this at least has survived, for to them this equality of spirit was precisely what was so precious to them.

Some older colonists will say though that the outright friendliness which was prevalent in their youth has diminished. They say that all strangers were greeted as friends whether on the lanes or in the home. There was no passing by without a word and doors were always open for anyone to enter. The children might go off in the morning to see someone, and they would be gone all day, staying for meals, and returning home at night. Judy Mardell recalls how her mother had a voice that carried, and when she wanted Judy home, she called, and wherever she might be, it was certain she would hear her.

It has also been admitted to me that the second generation were sometimes reluctant during their teenage years to admit that they came from Whiteway. As their homes were unconventional, it often made them feel different, and most youngsters like to be the same. 'It was all very well for our parents', one told me, 'they chose to come here, I couldn't.' This feeling has been replaced today, I can safely say, by a sense of pride. But then we are unique.

Vegetarianism, common to everyone here once, is not so widespread now, though, there are more here than in most villages. Today, though it has become more fashionable generally. Some colonists only eat a little meat, having been brought up in the old way, indulging infrequently in animal products. Judy always ate vegetarian fare at school, which was rather boring, as the wonderful variety which is available everywhere now, was unheard of then. It was cheese, nut rissoles and fried eggs then, and this monotonous offering turned her head a little, towards the variety available from the meat-based dishes.

Once a non-meat eater, ingrained from babyhood, it seems that it stays with you for life. Leonie's mother, Alice, on the other hand, did eat meat until, when staying at Whiteway House, pregnant with Leonie, she saw a freshly killed chicken hanging up and dripping blood. The queasiness felt then remained with her whenever she thought of meat, and she never indulged in it again, and neither did her daughter. It seems to me that vegetarians are basically a healthy lot, living long and active lives.

We have seen from a previous application letter how vegetarianism was important to life here, for many mention it, probably thinking that this would open the door to them and enable them to acquire some land. Those then did have strong feelings on how they wished to live their lives, most entirely genuine, and some just to escape from a drab or boring life.

We had an application the other day for land. It was quite satisfactory, but lacked the soul of hundreds I have read. It simply said they wanted to bring their children up in the country and Whiteway seemed a lovely place to do it!

Many came here to live as a result of holidaying here, after learning of its attitudes and vegetarianism. A typical example was Hilda Gustin. She had heard of Whiteway in 1935 while working at the Health Food stores in Oxford. She came to stay at Bidwell for a few weekends, and then at Nellie Shaw's from 1943. She went there several times, and when Nellie died, she stayed with Flossie Davies at the Retreat.

She recalls how Flossie was a born dramatist, and a wonderful talker, bringing all she said to life. Hilda and her son Michael would go for walks with Flossie's dog, Bob, down in Miserden Estate, and Michael would jump from mole hill to mole hill, in the field which stretched down to the stream.

It was while Hilda was working in London, that she enquired at the office of *Freedom Press* and Lilian Wolfe told her about a piece of land at Whiteway. After being granted her ground, she lived in a caravan from 1950 until her house, built by Jack Weston in 1954, could be completed. Her furniture was

*Flossie demonstrating spinning in August 1958.*

sparse, but she managed. The Colony life has suited her well, with its people and its history, much of which she learned when working with Gassy.

As stated previously there were no fences at one time, George Allen being one of the first to enclose his plot. All plots merged with their neighbours. Now it has become necessary for plots to be measured on exchange, if not previously done, so that all land holders know their limits, and will honour them. This would certainly go against those pioneering principles. It seems strange to learn that during the initial year here only six acres had been cultivated. Although people streamed here, to find this freedom that they all craved for, but was unattainable in their usual way of life, only the persistent in mind and body were prepared to sacrifice their previous comforts and stay.

People feel lost without rules. They are expected then to make their own within their consciences and many are unable to do this, so revert to the sanctuary of the normal world, where others will do it for them.

Those involved in the Whiteway experiment were not made to work, they were not made to do anything. That makes it hard. Even when results are forthcoming from physical effort, they do not always produce the satisfaction gained when it is done for oneself – because of wanting to do it. Francis said,

> How do we set people on equal footing? asks the visitor. There is no question of setting them on equal footing. Everybody must set himself there. And this can be done only by feeling in oneself . . . Only by forgetting the differences of opinion, profession, nationality, nay even sex, shall we all set ourselves on equal footing.

# *Chapter 25*

# HAS WHITEWAY SUCCEEDED?

What of those who left during that first year, what else did they do with their lives? Joseph Burtt, although only staying for a year took upon his shoulders all the financial problems which arose. The colony could not have done without him. His departure was not a complete abandonment though, for in later years he visited Whiteway often with his wife and two sons from his home in Derbyshire.

His life proved a fulfilling one, with him undertaking the investigation of slavery in Africa on behalf of a cocoa manufacturer, worried that slave labour was involved in the development of their product, and visits to Russia and the Near East for the Red Cross. This resulted in lectures and books written about the conditions found in these countries, as well as more light-hearted accounts on the native life and wild flowers found in these climates. So, although Whiteway did not serve to fill his life, at least it was the gap in the door which when opened fully, led to a far larger world with its problems.

Gospill, his brother, although in at the start, was really only a temporary member, as was Alec Protheroe, Sud's brother. Lucy Andrews having played her part during the Colony's most difficult time, left to get married, and Trafford upset those who had supported him by absconding without any warning in the summer of 1900 with twenty pounds and a box of clothes. Jack Bent the carpenter left in 1901 to return to whatever remained of Purleigh.

Sam Bracher whose inspiration and money made Whiteway Colony possible married Lottie as stated and lived in Sheepscombe for a time. Later he emigrated to New Zealand where, during the twenties, he became editor of an influential national daily paper. Lottie herself was a member of a well-known Yorkshire family and author of *The Standard Work of the League of Nations*. They stayed in New Zealand for several years and on their return Samuel became a Labour political correspondent.

Sudbury Protheroe remained at Salisbury with his second family, running his Fudge Shop, and never again returning to Whiteway to live. After his death on 9 December 1955, his wish that his ashes should return to the land of his youth, where love of his garden, honesty and thoroughness in his bakery business, and the memories of the social life in which he was always involved, would surround him once more, was fulfilled. A beech tree, which will always remain in remembrance of him was planted by Tom Keell Wolfe on the Old Children's Playground in a simple ceremony where all colonists gathered.

*Sud with his dog Mandy in front of Salisbury Cathedral in 1950.*

*Tom Keell Wolfe planting the beech tree in memory of Sudbury Protheroe, on the Old Children's Playground in 1955. John Evans brought the sappling up from the woods and Sud's ashes were scattered on its roots. It stands tall and fine today on the spot where the deeds were burnt by those early colonists to symbolise freedom from accepted convention.*

This has set a precedent for others who, having enjoyed life here wished that their memories might linger on the land of which they had been part.

Nellie Shaw's book on Whiteway when published, related the thirty odd early years, with the troubles and joys encountered. When Sam heard of it he contacted her, saying how glad he was that she had written Whiteway's story, and asking for forgiveness from her and all the old Colonists for his past actions, and saying how pleased he was that those traumatic first years had not caused it to fail.

It so happened that Joe Burtt, who was visiting his brother in Gloucester, and had come up to see his old friends on Whiteway while in the area, was at Nellie's on that July afternoon when the letter came, as were two old colony members Bea Adams and Jeannie Protheroe. Both Nellie and Joe wrote delightedly to him in return, and twice following that, letters were exchanged with promises that Sam would come to stay later in the year. Just as the time came round for his visit another letter arrived, stating that he was ill, and needed to be cared for in a nursing home. It was there that he died from cancer three weeks later, at only sixty years of age. Nellie writes,

> I attended the funeral, although it meant a long journey to Wincanton, Somerset, and met his brothers and sisters, who were extremely nice to me, having read the Whiteway book, and saying Sam had talked about me a good deal before his death. I feel so glad there was a reconciliation and Joe, whose bosom friend Sam had been almost wept with joy.

From all those early settlers the only family remaining to date are the Protheroes in the form of Sud's granddaughter, Jennifer. She still lives on the family plot in Meadow Cottage. But family structure is still very strong on Whiteway with at present about half the members being related to at least one other colonist. There are a number of large family groups which contain several generations, one of which links four families, and another five.

Such a network inevitably produces a family feel to the Colony as a whole. Qualities which go with a family structure have filtered through into Whiteway life more and more as the years passed by.

This is constantly being renewed as those small children, wishing to raise their own children in the same environment, return periodically, one day perhaps to remain permanently.

Many villages have expanded and been absorbed into the suburbs of towns. Whiteway has not, the farming area in which it stands limiting drastically its expansion. Children of every generation therefore grow up in the true country lifestyle.

A quarter of the Colony's population is retired, though not necessarily

*A group of colonists representing Whiteway in front of the Hall in October 1992. Pat Elliott, seated, Whiteway's oldest colonist at the time, died the following Dceember. (Photograph by Katrina Thacker)*

elderly. Some live alone, but many remain in couples, still young enough to be active, with a renewed freedom now that their family have left home. About half of those here are self-employed, with artists, a screen-printer and a metal worker, a garage owner whose success caused him to move to larger premises along the road but whose heart is still here, an 'earth mover' and a plantswoman-garden designer with a marvellous garden. There is also a nurse and a midwife, a teacher and an accountant, civil servants, one of whom is a prison warder, and shop-fitters, also several accomplished crochet- and needlewomen, and several other men in a variety of building trade skills. Those involved in the latter, usually repair our Whiteway houses, although many are built and maintained by the owners themselves. The elderly in particular are pleased to be able to have their neighbour do their repairs for them, as friends they trust and with whom they can chat.

All our older generation are looked upon with affection, and they are a pleasure to talk to with their youthful attitudes often belying their years.

The question is how can you quantify Whiteway's success. Those who forecast failure on the Colony's formation did so because of the way they viewed it. Francis Sedlak said that when one thinks of heaven on earth disappointment usually follows. He writes,

> People usually connect the word 'Colony' with the most fantastic pictures of the socialistic future, when all that grieves them nowadays will give place to a feeling of universal happiness. But as grievances vary from one individual to another, it is natural that everybody expects to find in a colony such a state of things as required for the realization of his own individual happiness. Thus instead of cosy homes they might find primitive huts, instead of rich stores for tomorrow but bare necessities for today.

In a symposium held in 1927 to examine Whiteway and its attitudes and functions, forty-seven contributions were read, with the result proclaiming that Whiteway would like to be viewed as an enlarged family as opposed to a miniature state, regulated and structured.

This enlarged family has come about in reality as some colonists are bound by family ties albeit retaining their own opinions and individuality whilst the rest expand these numbers by the sense of belonging that the Colony creates. In 1998, when a commendable one hundred eventful years will have passed, all here will once again unite in their hall where they will recall times past, of adversity and solidarity, happiness and sadness, while the symbol of their freedom, a bonfire, burns in memory of those long gone.

# INDEX

Illustration references are given in *italics* after text references.